Dating
with
Confidence

A Teen's Survival Guide

Jacqueline Jarosz

HOKAH PUBLIC LIBRARY
BOX 503 HOKAH, MN 55941
894-BOOK (2665)

Adams Media Corporation
Holbrook, Massachusetts

Copyright © 2000, Jacqueline Jarosz. All rights reserved.
This book, or parts thereof, may not be reproduced in any form
without permission from the publisher; exceptions are made for brief
excerpts used in published reviews.

Published by
Adams Media Corporation
260 Center Street, Holbrook, MA 02343. U.S.A.
www.adamsmedia.com

ISBN: 1-58062-293-3

Printed in Canada.

J I H G F E D C B A

Library of Congress Cataloging-in-Publication Data available
upon request from the publisher.

This publication is designed to provide accurate and authoritative information with
regard to the subject matter covered. It is sold with the understanding that the publisher is not engaged in rendering legal, accounting, or other professional advice. If
legal advice or other expert assistance is required, the services of a competent professional person should be sought.
— From a *Declaration of Principles* jointly adopted by a Committee of the American
Bar Association and a Committee of Publishers and Associations

This book is available at quantity discounts for bulk purchases.
For information, call 1-800-872-5627.

DEDICATION

To Milton C. Jarosz—who yelled at me for missing curfew and always asked, "Will there be any other girls there?" I miss you, Daddy.

ACKNOWLEDGMENTS

Much gratitude to Will, for giving me the opportunity of a lifetime. Special thanks to everyone who shared their unique first-dating experiences with me. I couldn't have done it without you!

And as always, for Arthur. My best date ever!

CONTENTS

INTRODUCTION

I remember my first date like it was yesterday, even though it obviously wasn't!

I was fifteen years old (somewhat ancient by today's standards) and had just finished my freshman year in high school. His name was Matt, and he was a senior. He had starred in our high school's production of the musical *Bye Bye Birdie*, and was, to my mind, totally and absolutely perfect. I spent a lot of hours hanging out near his locker, hoping to engage him in a brilliant conversation that would fully display my superior girlfriend qualities. Finally, after much manipulation and some harmless flirting, I got him to ask me out at the end of the school year. Of course, I said yes.

That's when the serious terror really began! Because, although I was psyched at the thought of going out on my first date, I was filled with anxiety about what the actual event would be like. What should I wear? Where will we go? What will happen? What will we talk about? Will he try to kiss me good-night? Will I let him? Will I like it?

Wait a minute—will my parents even let me go out on a date with a GUY! A guy with a moustache, no less? Will they be into the idea of me going out alone with a boy? This is just too much for me, I thought. Why don't I just stay home and watch *The Love Boat?*

Happily, my parents didn't have a problem with me going out on a date with a guy who had a moustache—turns out, our families went to the same church. So much for my sense of adventure and daring!

When the big night came, I looked pretty cool and confident. Luckily, only my parents had seen me just an hour earlier, rushing around the house announcing I had nothing to wear, and telling my dad he had to get me to the mall, pronto, or I would die of embarrassment, right there in the living room.

The result of all that stressing out? A very nice first date. Matt picked me up in his blue Buick, rang the doorbell, came inside and met my parents, then walked me to the car and opened my door for me. He took me to the movies and held my hand when the lights went down. When it ended, he took me out for a slice of pizza, then he brought me home. He walked me to my front door, gave me a very nice kiss goodnight, and that was that.

The next morning, my mom and grandmother both quizzed me. What happened? Where did he take you, and so on. My grandmother, who was always oh-so-helpful in stressful situations, told me Matt was too short for me. My mom told me she thought he had very nice teeth. I was too happy to mind their nosy questions. I was totally grown-up—I'd had my first date, and it had been a success.

Although Matt and I went out on subsequent dates, it was that first one—my first date ever—that remains burned into my memory. All the fear I felt, all the nervousness and excitement—every moment—will remain with me forever.

For most people, a first date is a definite milestone—something to both look forward to and fear. If you're lucky, you'll have someone to share these conflicting feelings with— a best friend, your mom, or another trusted confidant. If you're not—or you're too shy to do any sharing—you'll face these feelings alone.

First off—a word or two about dating.

Dating is a relatively modern-day experience. A century ago, the word did not even exist! Back then, when two people liked each other and wanted to get to know each other better, they engaged in a process called "courtship," which involved elaborate rituals, rules, and regulations. Men brought "courtship gifts" to the ladies they loved, things like flowers and handkerchiefs, and tried to prove their worthiness as an eligible mate for marriage. The courtship process was carefully regulated by the girl's parents, and "dates" were usually strictly chaperoned (and you get embarrassed when your mom tells you to be home by ten o'clock!). Actual dating, as we know it today, didn't become commonplace until the 1930s—and while that seems like a million years ago, it's still a pretty recent phenom, if you think about how long people have actually been living on this planet!

As recently as thirty years ago, people tended to get married at an earlier age—marriage between "high school sweethearts" was an everyday occurrence. So dating had even more significance than it does today. After all, the guy who was taking you to the soda shop for an ice cream soda might just be the guy you ended up marrying! There was also more formality involved in dating. Guys definitely had to come into the house to meet a girl's parents; girls wore extra-special outfits. And although the "double-date" was very popular, no one had ever heard of the phrase "group dating."

Today, first dates are often casual events (so are second and third dates, by the way). Although you might end up in a serious relationship, you also might end up being just good friends. If you go out on a first date, and decide you really can't stand the guy, you can brush it off and start all over again with someone new.

A first date can be a walk in the park, dinner and a movie, a day at the beach, or an afternoon at the mall. It can be a totally personal, one-on-one experience, just you and the one you like, or it can be a group activity, where a bunch of friends get together and spend time with one another. It can be romantic, with candlelight and soft music, or it can be loud, silly, and fun (hanging out at a batting cage or watching your school team win the football championship). It can the best night of your life, or totally, absolutely lame. But, it will be something you will always remember.

This book was created with you in mind, to help you face all the crazy emotions and practical issues (*Who pays for what? Who's going to drive?*) that surround your first date. It will also help you deal with those nasty self-esteem issues (*What if I ask him out—and he says no?*), answer questions about developing relationships (*My friends hate him, but I really like him. Should I date him?*), and even help you come up with inexpensive (but really special) ways to spend time with the one you like the most.

Since you're a very special person, you deserve to be treated in extra-special ways—this book will give you permission to expect the very best treatment from your dates. It will also give you the (unfortunately necessary) red flags—warning signs to let you know if the person you're dating is total bad news.

Finally, this book will talk about some of the very personal, physical issues of dating. When I went out on my first date, all I had to worry about was a goodnight kiss. Today's teens face more pressing, difficult questions about sex, and even more frightening issues about harassment and stalking. This book will give you the answers you need to make your decisions with confidence; it will also help you deal with problems that you might face.

The most important dating tip to remember is that dating is supposed to fun. Although you may find yourself going crazy, worrying and wondering about what the big day (or night) will bring, the bottom line is you should ultimately be enjoying yourself, spending time with someone you really like, getting to know someone, and sharing special times with them. That might not be enough to ease the quaking in your stomach or to stop your palms from sweating up when you walk out the door for your first date, but it is something you should always remember—dating is a fun, nice, enjoyable thing, and you and your date will have a much better time if you keep the worrying to an absolute minimum.

Another thing you should remember is this—anything can be a date! A walk in the park, a day at the beach, or a night at the movies—if you're spending quality time with someone you like, you're on a date! And that means a date should never be about money—like, "How much money did he (or she!) spend on me?" Dating should be about fun, and there are a million ways to have fun with someone you like. How much money a person spends on you is NOT the best way to judge how that person feels about you! In fact, the opposite is true—a truly creative, imaginative date that costs next to nothing really shows you how much you mean to another person; after all, why would someone go to all that trouble to plan the perfect date if he or she didn't really like you a lot.

Hopefully, this book will give you the 411 you need to kick back, relax, and have fun—well, after you've decided what you're going to wear, and argued with your parents about how late you want to stay out!

Oh, and in case you were wondering, Matt and I had a whole bunch of really cool dates together. Occasionally I still bump into him, and we're still able to smile about the good times and the memories we shared. And, he's still way shorter than I am and still has a moustache.

But that's another story. Right now, let's start talking about your first date, and the first question you need to ask yourself before you say "yes" to it. It's a very basic question, yet very few people really think about it before they jump into the dating game. That question is simply—Are you ready for it?

Your Questions, Your Answers

Before we start talking about your first date, let's talk a little bit about the types of questions you may have about dating in general.

When something is new to you, it's natural to have questions, concerns, and even some fears about it. Remember your first day of school? Chances are, you were a little nervous the night before; you might even have cried a little, or you might have told your parents you wanted to stay home with them. Once you got to school, you probably had an OK time—in fact, you probably forgot all your nervousness and fears and simply went about the business of learning and making new friends.

Or, what about the first time you ever played a sport on a team? The first time you played soccer, baseball, or basketball with a school or church team, you were probably a nervous wreck. You might even have gotten sick to your stomach. But once the game started, and you got involved in the action, you stopped feeling sick—you were too busy scoring goals, running the bases, or getting nothing but net.

You get the picture? Whenever you do something for the first time, it's scary. Especially when it's something you've built up in your mind—something that's important, new, and a very big deal. And that sounds like a first date to me.

Dating is a lot like that. It might seem scary—maybe even terrifying—but that's because it's something you've never done before. Once you're on your date, and you're laughing and enjoying yourself, you'll forget all about being nervous.

Another reason for the nervous pre-dating, sick-to-your-stomach feeling is that there's a lot of anticipation and expectation surrounding a first date. You've probably read magazine articles, listened to your friends talk about it, watched your favorite TV and movie characters tentatively step out into the dating world—chances are, you're already filled with anticipation for the day it will be your turn. And, you're probably filled with expectations, wondering what it will be like, how you'll look, what you'll say, and whether you'll be kissed goodnight!

There's absolutely nothing wrong with getting excited over your first date, your first boyfriend or girlfriend, your first romantic relationship, and your first kiss goodnight—it's totally natural to think about these things, and to fantasize about them in your daydreams. But with so much excitement and anticipation surrounding one single evening and event, it's no wonder you're filled with nervous dread. You may be thinking, "What if my first date doesn't live up to my expectations?" "What if my first date is a total flop?" Or worse still, "What if *I'm* a total flop?"

If you're getting ready to take the plunge into the dating world, it might be a good time to sit down and think about your expectations, your fears, and your concerns. What are some of the things you're most worried about? What are the issues you want cleared up in your mind?

Q *Am I ready to date?*
This is a serious question you have to ask yourself. It's also a question you're going to have to discuss with your parents or guardian. After all, they probably have some ground rules regarding dating, and it would be a good idea to know those ground rules in advance. Remember, being ready to date is more

than reaching a certain age or a certain grade; it has nothing to do with what your friends are doing, or what you think you *should* be doing. It's about being really ready—ready to deal with all aspects of dating, the fun parts, and the lousy parts.

Q How do I know if I like someone enough to go out on a date with him or her?

Chapter 3 of this book will help you decide if the person you've got your eye on is the person you want to spend more time with. Also, be sure and remember that going out on a date isn't a lifetime commitment—it's a date! A date is a way to help you decide if that special someone really is someone special. Chances are, if you enjoy someone's company and think they're cute and cool to hang with, you probably like them enough to date them.

Q How do I ask someone out?

This book will give you pointers on asking someone you like out on a date. And remember, boys and girls are both allowed to do the asking! If you're getting the jitters just reading this, remember that everyone gets nervous when they ask someone out on a date. You're not a freak because you get a queasy stomach when you think about asking out someone you like. The important thing is to get over that nervous feeling and just do it—after all, someone has to do the asking if a first date is going to occur.

Q What if I ask someone out, and he or she says no?

Rejection is rotten, no doubt about it, but rejection is a risk you are going to have to face whenever you ask someone out. And, whether you're thirteen or thirty-five, that risk is always going to be present. But fear of rejection is a seriously bad reason to not do that asking. Always remember, everyone gets rejected now and then throughout his or her life—that doesn't mean you shouldn't take the risk. Also remember that just because someone rejects you, it doesn't mean there's something wrong with you, so don't ever get down on yourself. If someone says no, it might just mean that person isn't right for you anyway.

Q *I've asked, she's said yes—now what?*
I've got a ton of suggestions for inexpensive, creative, and romantic dates. But if you use your imagination, I bet you can think up a hundred more. Remember, a date is supposed to be fun; it's a chance to get to know someone better, laugh a little, and enjoy someone's company—it's not an excuse to drain every penny out of your life savings. Have fun planning the date, and make sure to ask your intended what he or she enjoys—take a little time and you can create an extra special event your date won't ever forget.

Q *I don't drive yet. Does that mean I can't go out on a date?*
Nope. It just means you've got to be a little more creative about your date planning. You may have to have one of your (or your date's) parents pick you up and drop you off—lame, I know, but believe me, everyone goes through it, and it's not the worst thing in the world. There are some other alternative transportation methods, too—but being car-less shouldn't mean you're date-less.

Q *What happens after the date?*
If you had a great time, be sure to thank your date, and to tell your date how much fun it all was. If you had a lousy time, you should still thank your date for planning the day and for spending time with you. If, by "what happens?" you mean, do you get to kiss your date goodnight, that depends on whether or not the date went well, and whether or not you still like your date as much as you thought you did! If you're wondering how to treat the other person once you've been out on a date with

him or her, the answer is simple—treat him/her like the special person he/she is.

Q *What if my date had a great time and I had a rotten time? Or vice versa?*

It's always tough when a person likes you more than you like that person, or when you like someone more than he or she likes you. One of the things you're going to hear a lot about in this book is honesty—honesty is something that will help you in all aspects of your dating life. If someone likes you more than you like him or her, you've got to be honest and let him/her know. It sounds horrible, but it really solves lots of problems down the road. And if you like someone more than he/she likes you, you have to take a step back from the situation and not turn into a freaky stalker—that's definitely not going to make the person like you more!

Q *Does going out on a date mean I'm under obligation to have sex?*

It's amazing that some people still think this way, but the answer is a loud and unqualified NO! When you go out on a date, you're promising a date, not sex. If someone tries to force you or uses guilt (like, "I spent a lot of money for this date. I want something to show for it!"), get out and get away—this is totally unacceptable behavior, no exceptions!

Q *Is it OK to date more than one person at a time?*

Some people have no problem playing the field; some people prefer to take it one date, one person at a time. You'll have to decide what you're comfortable with.

These are just a few of the questions you might be thinking about, but you may have plenty more flying around your brain right now. Many of the answers to your questions will be addressed right here in this book; some you might want to discuss with your friends or family members. It's good to write down your questions, and to get them answered before you actually begin dating. That way, you'll feel more confident and sure of yourself.

Now let's get back to that first question—are you ready to start dating?

Are You Ready?

All your friends are doing it. Your big sister or older brother is doing it. And, it seems like everyone on TV and in the movies is doing it. What are you waiting for?

Shouldn't you be dating too?
Hold on a second! Take a deep breath. Chill and relax.
Let's talk about the facts.

CH-CH-CHANGES

As you've probably been noticing, your body has been going through some serious changes. In fact, your body is still changing, and probably will continue to do so for the next several years! A few years ago, you probably didn't even notice members of the opposite sex—except when it came time to make fun of them. Boys were totally yucky; girls had cooties—remember? If one of *them* accidentally rubbed against your shoulder while you were standing on the lunch line, it was cause for major screaming and maybe even some scrubbing when you got home.

Then somewhere along the line, things slowly began to change. For girls, the change starts earlier, usually between the ages of ten and thirteen; boys start a little bit later (that's why the phrase "Boys are so immature!" was invented). Girls begin to grow taller, and their bodies develop and mature; guys will notice their voices dropping an octave or two, and they'll start to see hair growing on their chins and cheeks. All these physical changes are a normal part of the growing process. You know it as "puberty," and it's probably driving you totally crazy right about now.

A lot of the changes are kind of gross—you might be experiencing some serious zit action on your face, and who the heck needs these cramps once a month? But all of these physical changes are adding up to a new, improved—and more grown-up—you.

Perhaps even more important than these physical changes are the changes going on inside your mind. Where boys were once yucky, now they are appealing; where girls were once cootie-ridden, now they're enjoyable company. Girls will gather together and giggle over boys they think are cute; boys will gather together and talk about their favorite girls. Slowly, girls and guys begin to engage in a process called "hanging out"—walking home from school together, talking quietly near a locker, sitting together at lunch time. They may then begin "going out," which may include activities like going to the movies, having dinner together, or getting together at sports events and parties. Going out may be an exclusive, one-on-one thing, or a group activity where a bunch of friends do things together (but where "couples" who clearly like one another pair off and spend time with each other). These tentative, early steps into the world of dating can be nerve-wracking, but since they're super-casual, and usually done in public (at school, at the mall, out on the street), they're not really threatening or scary. Early encounters with the opposite sex are really just extensions of the friend-making process—you're just getting to know someone new.

READY TO DATE? MAYBE, MAYBE NOT

Making a new friend and being ready to date him are two very different things. The question "Am I ready to date?" is a very complicated one, and what's worse—there are a whole bunch of people who want to "help" make your decision for you and with you.

Your Parents

When it comes to decisions about your first date, there are people who are even more interested in the outcome then you (and your potential date) are—your parents! That's right, those people who raised you, who help you with your homework, and drive you to soccer practice—those people you love a lot and fight with a lot. They're definitely going to want to have a major say in your dating decisions.

The first, and most important, thing you must learn to do with your parents is talk to them, honestly and openly, about your feelings. If you start talking at a young age, and feel comfortable being honest about what's going on in your world, you'll have a real head start for the dating conversation.

You should start talking to your parents as soon as possible, although it is definitely OK to wait for specific events to spur on the conversation. Here's a for example—your school is sponsoring a Valentine's Day dance, and you and your friends are planning to attend. Mom knows that, and she's already planning to take you dress shopping. Now let's say there's a guy in your class named Joey, and you think he is really, really cute. One day, after school, Joey asks if he can "take you" to the dance. ("Take you" is in quotes because actually someone else may be doing the "taking"—the driving, that is. More on that later!) Anyway, you walk home from school and you're walking on air—the guy of your dreams has just asked you out! But first, you gotta tell your parents, who've been under the assumption that they're driving you (and your friends) to the dance and picking you up themselves. Since you're going to the dance already, this situation is the perfect opportunity for a full, serious, and intense conversation with your 'rents concerning dating.

Of course, when you tell your mom the good news about the dance and the boy of your dreams, you really shouldn't be surprised if she just says, "NO WAY!" The truth is, most parents aren't prepared for the start of their teenager's "dating season"—they probably figured you wouldn't start dating until you were well out of college! Their initial reaction to your total happiness may be total unhappiness.

It's sometimes hard for parents to understand that you're growing up. They might still think of you as their little baby, and the thought of you walking out their front door with a member of the opposite sex might be more than they can handle.

And never forget, your parents' number one, most important job is taking care of you and making sure you're safe. They might be absolutely terrified at the prospect of you going out with a stranger—it's a dangerous world out there, after all, and your parents might be thinking the worst right now.

This is the time to talk to your parents about the practical side of dating—like, at what age can you start? Many adults think that a teen should wait until he or she is sixteen before exclusive, one-on-one dating begins. In some families, that number may be even higher, like eighteen.

Before you run away screaming and crying, remember that screaming and crying will NOT get you to the dance with Joey. And, it definitely won't inspire a serious dating discussion with your parents—something you need to have if you're going to get all the information you need.

The reason your parents don't want you to go out on an exclusive, one-on-one date with Joey is they think you're too young; they think you're too immature; or they're not into staying up all night worrying about what you're doing. They also might be concerned about you embarking on a relationship that might turn serious. Screaming and crying will make them think their first two concerns are right on target.

Whenever you're having serious discussions with your parents, don't whine! No matter how upset and nervous you are, do not whine, ever. Whining says you're still a little kid.

The best way to deal with parents is to always remain reasonable. Ask them what they think about "group dating," where couples go out together, in a big group. This type of dating (which we'll talk about in a later chapter) is a more casual, low-key situation, and most parents will permit that type of activity—especially if another parent, or a group of parents, are involved in driving you and your friends wherever you want to go. That, by the way, helps take care of the "staying up all night worrying" problem.

As for their last concern, their worries about this becoming a "serious" relationship, that's a problem. No matter how hard you try to convince your 'rents that "it's just a date," they're going to worry about what that one date could lead to. They might be worried that you might become very serious, that you might put the person you're dating in front of school and your future. And they're probably worried that you might start experimenting with sex. These are major concerns for your parents.

The most important thing to remember about parents and dating is this—they're really concerned only about your safety and welfare, and they're not trying to hurt you or totally screw up your social life. But to keep from getting into huge fights all the time, it's vital that you sit down with them and find out exactly what you can expect in the future.

What you need to know is, at what age will you be allowed to go out on a one-on-one date? If that age is still a couple of years away, at what age can you start going out in groups or on group dates? When you *are* allowed to date, what will they (your parents) expect from you, behavior-wise? For example, will they want to meet the guy before you walk off into the world with him (most will); will they expect you to leave a phone number where you can be reached (some will); will they expect you to be home by 8:30 P.M. (most won't, but you never know!).

Another thing you should probably know—the "experts" who study stuff like teenage dating all seem to agree that sixteen is the best age to begin one-on-one dating. They say it's the age when you're emotionally mature enough to deal with exclusive relationships—seeing one person, and one person only. But group dating is another story, and these same experts say that thirteen or fourteen is a fine age to begin interacting socially with members of the opposite sex. So be prepared, because your parents are probably going to want you to wait.

So what about Joey, your big date for the dance? Well, you've still got some reading to do—we'll get back to him later!

My parents won't let me date— so what do I do now?

A lot of parents really put their collective feet down when it comes to dating—and those feet usually mean a total stamping out of your social life! If your mom and dad are dead-set against you dating, there are a few, reasonable things you can do to change their minds.

Urge your parents to talks to your friends' parents!

Have you ever said the following to your parents: "But everybody else is doing it!" What about, "But Jennifer can stay out until midnight! Why can't I?"

Is everybody else doing it? If your friends really do have less strict curfews or more lenient dating privileges, why not get your mom and Jennifer's mom together so they can talk about it? Your parents might be more likely to give you more freedom if they know other parents are doing it, and are comfortable with it.

If, however, you are lying, and Jennifer's curfew is actually one hour earlier than yours, avoid this tactic altogether. And if nobody else really is doing it, then why not chill out and stop stressing about dating for now?

Keep it casual!

Lots of parents worry about their teens getting involved in way-too-serious relationships at a young age. That's why so many 'rents keep their kids out of the dating loop for so long.

If you and your friends are starting to go out on group dates, stress to your parents that it's a total social occasion—not a prelude to an early walk down the aisle. Let your parents know that you just want to have fun with friends, and that going out on your first date does not mean that you've committed to someone for the rest of your life.

Of course, some parents believe that your first date automatically leads to your first sexual encounter (we'll talk about that in a later chapter, by the way). "Serious" is your parents' code word for sex, something they would really prefer you wait for. Thus, they figure, if they can postpone your first date, they can postpone your introduction to sexual issues.

Again, stress that your first date will be a fun social occasion rather than a "serious" one. Let your parents know that you are a responsible person and that you're perfectly comfortable keeping things casual. Ask them if they'd consider group dating or double-dating—they might be more comfortable knowing you're with a group of people, 'cause most parents do agree with the old cliché "there's safety in numbers."

Show off your sense of responsibility!

Are you home when you say you're going to be home? When you're given a chore, do you complete it? Do you do your homework? Do you work hard to be all you can be at school? Do you see what I'm getting at?

If you exhibit responsible behavior, you will ultimately be given more responsibility. If you show your parents that you can be trusted, they will be more likely to trust you. It's a lot simpler than the stuff you're currently learning in geometry, isn't it?

If you tell your 'rents you're going to be at the library, and they later find out you've been spending your afternoons at the mall, they're not going to trust you—ever! Believe me, once you start to lose your parents' trust, you rarely regain it completely again. And believe me—parents always find out when you tell a lie. It's some sort of wacky parent ESP—they always find out. It's always better to play it straight with your parents—it solves a lot of problems in the long run.

The bottom line—and I can't say it enough—is this: if you want your family to treat you with respect, and you want them to give you more responsibility, then act responsibly!

Be realistic in your expectations!

If your parents have totally forbidden you to date until you're sixteen, it's probably unrealistic to expect them to change the age restriction to thirteen, don't you think? But they might agree to a compromise—say, perhaps, letting you date when you're fifteen! Try to reason with your parents in a calm manner, and see if they'll do a little bending—but again, don't push them too much. You want to go out on a date SOMETIME THIS CENTURY!

Don't compare yourself to your sibs!

So your older brother went out on his first date when he was twelve. Now your parents tell you that you have to wait until you're sixteen. This is parent logic at its worst, isn't it?

Although your parents will probably tell you how "fair" they are when it comes to dealing with siblings, the fact is there will be some differences between how they treat your sibs and how they treat you. Some families treat boys differently from the way they treat girls. Some parents might be more lenient with the first child and stricter with the baby of the family. Or maybe your older sister did something really rotten on her first date and spoiled it for you.

Is this fair? No! But pointing out the unfair situation will not make it go away. The fact is, your parents will not be able to explain why your brother had permission to date when he was twelve while you have to wait. And questioning them further will probably just annoy them.

Another fact is that you don't know the whys and wherefores of the situation either. Perhaps they were more lenient with him and he took advantage of it. Perhaps they thought he could handle it, and they think you can't. Whatever! The point is, it's not going to change, no matter how many times you say, "You let Michael get away with everything!"

Enjoy your social life with your friends!

This might seem like it doesn't fit in here, but it really does. The fact is, your parents may lay down the dating law, and it may not be in your favor. So, are you going to sit in your room and mope until you're sixteen? Think again! If your parents really won't budge on the dating issue, the best thing to do is simply have fun with your friends and enjoy your life. Spend time with them and keep up a positive attitude. If you're someone who enjoys life now, you can rest assured you'll have plenty of dating offers in the future—everyone likes a person who's always smiling and making the most of life. So don't mope—you're dating time will come soon enough.

I still think I'm ready— so I'll sneak out and date

If you had this reaction to the previous section, then you're really too immature to be thinking about dating. You should probably stick to video games. This is *such* a majorly bad idea!

Under no circumstances should you ever, ever sneak out to meet a date. Nor should you ever lie to your parents—you know, like telling them you'll be at the library when you're really meeting your crush at the mall. It may seem like a harmless, white lie, but it's really the little stone that will start an avalanche of distrust. Once you've lied to your parents, they'll never forget it, and rebuilding those bonds of trust could take years.

More importantly though, sneaking out and telling your parents you'll be at one place when you're really planning to go to another is a recipe for disaster of the really dangerous kind. It's always majorly vital that your parents know where you are, just in case something bad happens to you, like an accident.

If you've really got a problem with your parents' rules and regulations, the best way to deal is to talk with them, and to constantly reinforce how trustworthy and mature you really are. In the long run, building this bridge of trust between you and your parents will yield wonderful results—and will help you gain a ton of independence.

If you're thinking, "Hey, if I sneak out, my parents will never know!"—trust me, they'll know. And you might find yourself sitting home watching *Nick at Nite* until you're well over thirty-five years old.

Your Friends

Other than your parents, there's another group of people that's probably taking a keen interest in your dating habits— your best buds, your true blues, your closest friends, of course.

And the interest is mutual! You've probably been keeping a very close eye on what your buds are doing, dating-wise. If fact, you may have already uttered this world-famous phrase to your parents: "But all my friends are already dating!"

Friends are a great source of information—you tell each other everything, about everything. If one of your friends has been out on a date already, chances are you've already heard every last detail down to the goodnight kiss. A few of your friends might already be involved in "serious relationships," and you might be feeling envious or left out.

While your best friend is definitely someone you'll want to share straight talk with, beware of sharing too much with too many people. If you've got questions your best friend can answer, that's most excellent. But not everyone in your crew may be as honest and truthful as your best friend will be. Both boys and girls aren't always 100 percent honest about their romantic experiences, so be sure and take everything you're hearing with a grain of salt.

Want a for example? Here's one—one of your acquaintances at school has been telling you about the older girl he's been seeing, the one who goes to high school in a town about 30 miles away. You may be envious of him, curious about it, or even a little annoyed about your lack of a girlfriend. And guess what? THERE MAY BE NO GIRL 30 MILES AWAY! He may be lying through his teeth, trying to impress and annoy you!

Here's another example? A girl in your class has been gabbing away about the boy she met while she was on vacation. As she spins her tale of summer love, you may find yourself feeling jealous or left out—hey, the only guy you saw this summer was your little brother, and he still dribbles food all over himself! But guess what? The only guy SHE saw this summer was her OLDER brother—who might not drool, but is still not the hot summer romance she's been describing.

And another example—sorry dudes, but it's true—guys tend to lie about sex and physical stuff, a lot. In fact, when guys are talking to their guy friends about getting busy, they're almost always lying. It must be something in the guy genes, 'cause it's been happening since time began. Don't take it personally though—just be aware of it! (And maybe you can be the guy to put an end to it!)

Why do friends and—more often—acquaintances lie? To get attention, of course! That's a no-brainer. Isn't that why you do goofy things like that sometimes?

That's why you need to reserve your serious dating conversation for your closest friends, the ones you trust the most, and the ones you know will not throw you a line of garbage when you're looking for information. Serious talks with close friends

LOUISE'S STORY: READY OR NOT

"My first date was terrible. It was the eve of our eighth grade dance, and these three poor little dweebs asked me and my two best girlfriends out. It was a very big deal to have a 'boyfriend' for the dance. My date's name was Russ, and he took me out once before—we went out for ice cream, and truthfully, I was so not into him. But he liked me, and I wanted to have a boyfriend for the dance. Was I ready to date? Absolutely not! My friends all pressured each other to go out with the three guys. I guess I learned that if you really don't like the guy, there's really no sense in going out with him, because it only hurts his feelings. Poor little Russ!"

will help you determine if you, and they, are ready to really start getting serious about dating.

And if you're not ready? Like I said before, there are plenty of things you and your friends can do together that don't involve dating. And while you're doing them, you can still gossip like crazy about your crush.

You

Yes, you're the most important person on this list. You really need to think about the prospect of dating— what it means and what it'll mean to you.

Before you consider going out on your first date, sit down at your desk, pull out a piece of paper and a pen, and make a list of the pros and cons of dating. Of course, the pros could include things like, "All my friends are doing it" or "I really, really, REALLY like this guy in my algebra class, and I think it would be really fun to go out with him." But, how about the cons?

✔ If I start dating, I might not have time for all the activities I love so much, like playing tennis or acting in the school play.
✔ If I start dating, I might not have time to do my homework and my grades might suffer.

Dating with Confidence

- ✔ If I start dating one person exclusively, I'll miss out on getting to know all the people I haven't met yet.
- ✔ My best friend isn't dating anyone yet—I wouldn't want to lose the close bond I have with her.

See, there are plenty of cons—and I bet you can think of quite a few of your own. The truth is, you might not be ready for dating at all, and you may *know* you're not ready. So before you start jumping into the dating pool with both feet, remember to take some time and think about how you really feel about it. You might realize that waiting to date isn't the worst thing in the world. In fact, it might just be the perfect choice for you.

Avoiding the dateless blues

Whether you're not dating by choice, or because no one's asked you yet, it can sometimes be a drag not to be involved in the dating scene. You might feel resentful of your friends who are dating, or you might start thinking negative thoughts about yourself, like "I'm never going to get asked out!" or "I guess I'm just a loser 'cause no one likes me."

TOM'S STORY: TO DATE OR NOT TO DATE?

"I was in sixth grade, and everyone in my crew seemed to have a girl-friend—but I didn't! I was so embarrassed about it that I made up a story that I was seeing someone in another state! I don't really think any of them believed me. Finally, I asked out a girl in my class. I went up to her and said, 'Do you want to be my girlfriend?' and she said 'Yes.' And that was it! I think we walked home from school together a few times, and held hands. I definitely was not ready for a girlfriend—I didn't even know what 'dating' meant."

Remember that if you don't like yourself, it's going to be hard for anyone else to. Treat yourself well and stay positive—believe me, you will find someone who likes you, and one day you'll join the dating brigade. There's no reason to get the blahs just because you're a single person; remember, positive and upbeat people tend to be more attractive, and they have more fun in the long run.

I've Got a Crush on You

3

HOW TO TELL IF YOU'RE REALLY IN "LIKE"

You just can't stop thinking about that guy in your math class. You find yourself daydreaming about the girl who sits behind you on the bus. You're in the first row at every single school soccer game, just so you can stare at the dude who tends goal. Every time you see the head cheerleader, you get a sick, queasy feeling in your stomach.

Guess what? You've got a serious crush! Actually, a "serious crush" is a total oxymoron, because the actual definition of "crush" is "an infatuation, usually passing." In other words, no matter how serious your crush is, it'll eventually fade.

Right! The key word being "eventually." I suffered through a four-year high school crush on Jerry, who played the sax in the school band. It started when I was freshman and ended some time after graduation. For four long years, I suffered the following crush symptoms:

✔ Queasy stomach every time we were in the same room.
✔ An inability to complete a sentence while speaking to him.

✔ Utter rage whenever I saw him hanging out with another female—even if that female was our geometry teacher!

✔ A constant state of hope that one day he would notice me and ask me out.

He didn't, and I totally survived—but those were four tough years.

A key to understanding crushes is this—most crushes are focused on people you don't know that well. For example, you may be crushing on the guy in your math class—even though you've never exchanged two words with him. Or, you may have a little thang for the head cheerleader just because she once said "hi" while passing you in the hallway. Crushes can be based on physical (he's cute; she's got a great smile) or non-physical (he's an incredible guitar player; she has such an awesome sense of humor) attraction, but they're missing something majorly important—something called reality!

Crushes That Crush You

There's absolutely nothing wrong with having a crush on someone—crushes are fun, exciting, and almost totally harmless. It's seriously fun to see the guy you're crushing on hanging out in the hallway, to watch him play basketball, and to hope he'll notice you and smile or say something nice. It's exciting when your crush object shows up at the mall at the same time you just happen to be strolling past the Coconuts Record Store—and you both walk in at the same time and head toward the same rack of CDs!

But, a crush can also bring you a lot of disappointment and pain, especially if you get too emotionally involved in it. If your crush object starts dating someone else, for example, you might actually feel as much pain as if you were dating him exclusively! But, even little things can hurt you: if he continuously ignores you, if she says "hi" to your best friend and not to you, even if he leaves class early to go to the

STAR CRUSHES

If you ever had a crush on a celebrity from TV, movies, or the pop music scene—join the club! Just about everyone on the planet has had a crush on a star at one time or another. In fact, that's why magazines such as *16* or *SuperTeen* were born—to bring you up-to-the-second information about the hot celebrity you're crushing on, as well as the coolest pictures you can hang on your wall or in your locker at school.

Crushes on celebs are more than just a lot of fun—they're very important to your development and maturation process! They help you determine exactly what qualities (physical, emotional, etc.) you like in someone else. While you were hanging up pin-ups and posters of your favorite singer (so his face would be the last thing you saw before floating off to sleep), you were actually learning something pretty important!

You might even be able to see how your old crush-choices translate into your current guy or girl "type." Do you favor the "shy guy," "the boy-next-door," or "the wild one"? If you look back at the stars you idolized in days gone by, you might be able to see that those qualities were evident in the celebs whose photos adorned your walls.

doctor—how dare he leave before you got the full day's dose of him?

If your heart is aching over a crush, it's definitely time to sit back and assess the situation. It may be time to start getting involved in other activities until your intense feelings pass. After all, going crazy over an unattainable crush is a little . . . crazy.

In a later chapter, I'll be filling you in on some of the wild—and sometimes scary—things people do when a crush gets crazy. For now, let's concentrate on turning your crush into a like-object.

CLOSE TO HOME CRUSH

There is another type of crush, but this type actually falls a little closer into the category of "really liking someone"—that's the crush you have on someone you do know, someone who's a little "closer to home." It might be the guy who lives next door to you, who you've known since you were three; it might be the girl who's the daughter of your parents' best friends; it might be someone you know from church or temple, someone you see often and are actually pretty buddy-buddy with.

If you've got a secret crush on someone you're close to, someone you already know pretty well, you're in luck—you've already got a good relationship with the person, and he/she already knows you're alive! This is the type of crush that can lead to a real relationship one day.

Of course, crushes like these can still be way one-sided. The other person might know you're alive, but might not particularly care (harsh, huh?). But, you're still in good shape, because the more you interact with your crush, the more you learn about him or her—and the more he or she learns about you. You have a real opportunity to decide if this person is someone you really, really like.

When a Crush Turns into a "Like-Object"

So when does a crush officially turn into a "like-object"?

✔ When you've actually exchanged a few words, and your crush knows your name.

✔ When you know a little bit more about your crush—like his favorite music or her favorite sport.

✔ When the crush starts seeking *you* out for conversation!

✔ When you're comfortable in the presence of your crush—you can speak without sputtering, stand there without sweating, and smile with confidence knowing *you're* pretty special too.

Common Ground

Ever hear the phrase "opposites attract"? It basically means that two people who are very different (in their opinions, beliefs, and even what they like to do for fun) can still be very attracted to one another and, in some cases, enjoy very nice romantic relationships. Truth is, it's not always true.

But, you're thinking, it has to be true. It's a saying!

Here's the absolute truth—it's much nicer when the person you like likes the things you like. In fact, one of the things that often turns a crush into a serious like-object is the presence of common interests.

Think about it! He likes football, she doesn't. She likes reading mystery novels, he doesn't. He loves Burger King hamburgers, she likes Wendy's. She likes hip-hop, he likes alternative. This relationship is going nowhere fast. The two of them have absolutely nothing to talk about, nothing to enjoy together.

I once dated a guy named Scott who really liked Sylvester Stallone movies. I mean, he really, really liked Sylvester Stallone movies. Now, there's nothing wrong with Sylvester Stallone movies—but there are other movies out there that don't star Sylvester Stallone. Not for Scott. He wouldn't step foot into a movie theater unless a Sylvester Stallone movie was playing. Eventually, this got very old.

You see what I'm getting at? No matter how cute your crush is, you're going to get very tired of him or her if you don't have some common interests to share.

The good news is, anything can be a common interest! Music, sports, books, movies, *Star Wars* memorabilia—if you both like it, it's a common interest, and it's a great start to building a friendship.

Think about your closest friends. The things that make them your closet friends are the things you share together. You hang out together, talk, shop, whatever—the key of common interests opens the door to the most lasting friendships. And, a solid friendship is one of the things that will help graduate your crush into a full-fledged like-object.

Did I lose you back at "opposites attract"? Are you still wondering if there's any truth to that saying? The answer is—sometimes yes, sometimes no. There are couples who swear each member of the pair is the total opposite of the other. But if you look closely, I'll bet you'll find that these couples share a lot of values and beliefs—even if one prefers Burger King and the other Wendy's. After all, opposites may attract, but common interests and ideals are the glue that binds relationships together.

The Comfort Zone

For just a second, stop reading and think about your favorite pair of shoes. Why are they your favorite pair? Could it be because they feel really good on your feet? Because you can walk for miles in them and never develop a single blister? Because they fit well and look great at the same time?

Those shoes fall into your comfort zone, and as a result, you totally love them, and wear them every day. So what's that got to do with your crush or like-object?

Everything! Because when you're comfortable around your crush, you've got the makings of a great relationship.

Remember Jerry, the guy from the band? Whenever I saw him, I felt like I was going to lose lunch (or breakfast, depending on the time of day!). During my sophomore and senior years, I saw him seven times a day because we had every single class together—that made for some serious Maalox moments!

I never, ever felt comfortable around him. I was never able to just walk up to him and start a cool conversation. I couldn't—I was too busy shaking with nerves. That's why he was always a crush, not a true like-object.

One of the reasons a crush is so exciting is because of the nervous way your crush makes you feel. But, that nervous feeling alone is not enough to ensure a great like-object. The key is comfort; and comfort comes when you're able to really relax and be yourself.

A Word on the Cyber World

Chat rooms and Internet relationships fall into the category of "things I didn't have to deal with when I was a teenager." I know, the dark ages again!

These days, lots of young people meet other young people in chat rooms on the Internet. It's a very cool way to get to know people from faraway places, and it's definitely a neat way to make new friends. But sometimes, when you're chatting, you find something you may not have been looking for—a crush!

You've probably already heard all the warnings about cyberspace, but I think it might be a good idea to mention something about it here. Remember that the person you're chatting with is a perfect stranger, no matter how often you've logged on together. You really don't know what this other person is like—you may not even know what they look like. There's always the possibility that the person on the other end of the computer screen is completely scamming you. Make sure you never give out any personal info, like your phone number or your address, to anyone on the Net— use your head so you don't get into any cyber-trouble.

KIM'S FIRST CRUSH: THE CUTEST THING

"My very first crush was Casey, in the first and second grade. He was really, really cute—he had blonde hair and green eyes, and these big lips. We sat at little tables, and he sat in front of me, and I could watch him and see his profile all the time—he was the cutest thing. He was a really good student, so I wanted to be even better, so we would have something in common. And on Halloween, I specifically went to his house to see what his mother was giving out. She was sitting on the stoop with this big bowl of candy, and I thought she was so cool. But he never noticed me. And he grew up to be a big jerk."

CRAIG'S CRUSH TIMES TWO

"I once had crushes on two girls at the same time! One girl was in band with me, and the other was in my algebra class. I couldn't figure out who I liked more. So I asked out the girl from the band, and she said no. Then I asked out the girl from algebra and she said yes, and we dated for about two years. I remember I felt so bad that she hadn't been my first choice—but of course I never told her that!"

Being You

This is the first, but definitely not the last, time I'll be telling you about the importance of being yourself. The reason those shoes are so comfortable is because you can relax when you're wearing them. Being happy with yourself and giving yourself permission to relax around your crush will ease that nervous feeling and allow a friendship to develop naturally.

Remember, if your crush doesn't like you the way you are, then he's a loser and not worth wasting your time over. Someone who truly likes you for the special person you are is the one worth having!

Am I boring you with the Jerry story? I thought you might like to hear the end of it. During our senior year, he started dating this girl named Fran, who had the biggest hair ever. And guess what? I got over it.

Once you're comfortable around your crush—comfortable enough to let the real beauty of your personality and inner self shine through—you'll know you've got yourself a genuine like-object. And you're probably going to start thinking about how nice it would be to share a date with this person.

Yikes!

Don't worry—the first date is always the toughest! And we're going to help you get through it in style!

Ask and You Shall Receive

4

Asking someone out on a date is like a box of chocolates—you really, truly never know what you're going to get. I sure hope Forrest Gump accepts my apologies for stealing his line, but never has a statement been more true. Asking someone out on a date is a total mystery—right up until the person gives you their answer.

Even when you absolutely, positively know that someone likes you, that person still might say no to a date! It may not even have anything to do with you! Maybe that person isn't allowed to date yet. Maybe they have a boyfriend or girlfriend in another school. Or, maybe they just really aren't into the dating scene at this very moment—they might be too into sports or academics, and not terribly interested in getting involved with someone.

Yes, asking someone for a date can be like walking on treacherous ground. But if someone doesn't do the asking, no one is going to be doing the dating.

BOYS AND GIRLS DO IT

It wasn't that long ago that only guys knew about the queasy stomach, sweaty palms, and general nervousness that comes over you when you're getting ready to ask someone for a date. That's 'cause in the old days, only guys did the asking. Girls never, ever asked a guy out on a date. In fact, girls were discouraged from even showing an interest in a guy—playing hard to get was something every girl learned to do.

But nowadays, it's much more common to see girls asking out guys. It's more common—but it's still not the absolute norm. There are still lots of guys who think a girl who does the asking is too aggressive, too forward, and too, well, masculine. (And there are a lot of girls who think the same thing!) There are also boys who *say* it's OK for a girl to do the asking, then freak out when it actually happens.

But, there are also plenty of guys who think it's awesome when a girl asks them out—hey, it saves them the nervous, quivery stomach, doesn't it! Also, it takes confidence for a girl to ask out a guy—and confidence is a trait lots of guys think is really attractive.

The problem for a girl is, she doesn't know which type of guy she's dealing with until she actually asks! So should she or shouldn't she becomes an overwhelming question.

The thing is—if a guy is creeped out or scared off by a girl who's confident enough to ask him out, then he's probably a guy who has a head full of insecurities and hang-ups. He might be the type of guy who still believes that girls have their "place"; he might think girls shouldn't play sports or have career aspirations either. He might be what used to be called a male chauvinist pig. Who wants to deal with that, really?

The bottom line is that it *does* take guts to ask someone out, whether you're a guy or a girl. It takes nerves of steel to walk up to the person you like and ask him or her for a date. But asking is the first step to a most excellent time and possibly even a boyfriend-girlfriend relationship. So, it's definitely worth the risk and the nerves—GO FOR IT!

Dating with Confidence

HOW SHOULD YOU ASK?

Don't you sometimes wish you had a script—just like they do in the movies and on TV—to help you know exactly what to say in all situations? One thing's for certain—when it comes to asking someone out, it's definitely helpful to plan out what you're going to say beforehand!

Asking someone out is one of those weird situations—you don't want to make a big, huge, overdone deal over it (just in case the person you ask says no), but you don't want it to be a casual question either. You want to show the person that you've thought about it, that this is something important to you. But you also don't want to sound desperate. Tough balance—but you can do it!

There are several ways you can ask someone out. Hopefully, you'll find a script that fits your personality and asking style.

"Would you like to come with me?"

When you're asking someone out on a date, it's always helpful to have a set plan, and nothing helps that plan come together like a set activity or event. If you know your like-object enjoys soccer, for example, you can ask him or her to a soccer game. If you know your crush is into culture, you can ask him or her to see a school play or to visit a museum with you.

Here's the way you ask:

"I've got an extra ticket to the big soccer game this weekend. Would you like to come with me?"

Or:

"I've got two tickets to the school musical. Would you like to come with me?"

The phrase "would you like to come with me" makes it clear you're asking someone out for a date. But because you've already got the tickets, and you've already made the plans, the whole asking process becomes a little more relaxed and casual. See?

If you're really, really nervous about asking someone out, this option offers an extra-cool way to calm you—you can use it as an "alibi." Here's what I mean—go up to your like-object and say, "My friend and I were supposed to go to this concert together, but he/she cancelled and now I have this extra ticket. Would you like to go with me?" Not only does this make you look social and popular, but it will also make your potential date feel good about accepting—after all, someone else wanted to hang with you, you must be OK, right?

"Would you like to come along?"

Another easy, laid-back way to ask someone out is to ask him or her to accompany you and your friends to an event. (You can read more about group dating and how it all works at the end of this chapter!) If you and your crew are planning an afternoon or an evening out, you can ask your like-object to join you—how easy is that?

Here's the way you ask:

"My friends and I are all going to catch that new Jim Carrey movie at the ten-plex. Would you like to come along?"

Or:

"A bunch of us are going to get something to eat after the game. Would you like to come along?"

Again, it's clear you want to spend time with the person, but the way the question is phrased keeps it all on a casual plane. And by asking your date out for a group activity, you make it clear that the date is going to be casual and social—which might make your like-object more likely (and more able, if he or she has parents who allow only group dating) to say yes.

"Would you like to go to the . . . with me?"

This is where we get into a little more nerve-inducing territory, 'cause this is where you're actually asking someone to go out with you—and you alone. If the person says yes, you've got a date to plan; if the person says no, you've got to handle the feelings of rejection.

Always remember that everyone gets nervous when they ask someone they like for a date—even your favorite celebrities get the jitters. So don't worry about being nervous— it's natural and it's to be expected. Just be prepared—figure out exactly when and where you're going to do the asking and then do it. Plan what you're going to say, take a few deep breaths and go for it.

Here's how you ask:

"I was wondering if you'd like to go to the movies with me on Saturday night."

Or:

"I was hoping you'd come to the school dance with me."

You can even get away with the sort of lame . . .

"I was wondering if you'd like to get together and do something with me on Saturday night."

(That last one is lame because it's always better to have an idea of what you'd like to do, and to present that idea to your date-to-be. With that last one, it's quite possible you're inviting your like-object to come over and wash your father's car.)

Asking someone out this way is definitely more intense. It's clear it's just going to be the two of you, and it's an invitation for a more formal, proper type of date. But don't worry—you're up to the challenge. Just go for it.

A must to avoid . . . "You want to go out with me?"

Whatever you do, do NOT ask your like-object the following question:

"So, you want to go out with me?"

What does this question mean? Does it mean, "Do you want to go out . . . ever?" Or does it mean, "Do you want to go out with me to the supermarket?"

You see what I'm saying. The person you're asking might say no because they haven't the foggiest idea what you're talking about!

Whenever you ask someone out, remember to be specific! Ask someone to an event, or to join you in an activity.

GO FOR IT

As I've said, asking someone out on a date is a stomach-twinging, palm-sweating, spine-tingling proposition. There are two things that make the date-asking process so scary—and the first one is that horrible question, "How do I avoid making a fool of myself?" (The second scary thing is the possibility of rejection—we'll talk more about that in a little while.)

It's absolutely, totally normal to be afraid of embarrassing yourself. Being afraid of making a fool of yourself is the number one reason people don't try new things—they're afraid of being embarrassed, of looking silly, of having people make fun of them. The thing is, if you worry about it too much, you end up missing a lot of the fun things life has to offer. If you're cool enough to risk being embarrassed, you'll end up having a lot of great times throughout your life.

Still, it's a major roadblock isn't it, that fear of being embarrassed. It's tough to get up the confidence to take that risk, plunge forward, and try something new. How are you supposed to do it?

I won't tell you it's easy, but it is possible to get over your fear of looking foolish. Your first step is to remember that the person you're asking out is a human being, just like you are. He or she has feelings and concerns and issues of his/her own. Your like object is probably just as worried about keeping his/her coolness as you are. Always remember, no matter how hot your like-object is, he or she really is just a person, not a superhero. There's nothing to fear in approaching your like-object and asking himr or her out.

The second thing you should remember is that you have a lot to offer as a potential date. You've got great, positive qualities that you should be proud of, and pleased to share with others. There's nothing foolish about you—you're a good person with a good heart, and if you're confident about yourself, there's nothing in the world that can stop you from reaching your goals. Nothing except you. So remember your good qualities, and think about them when you're asking someone out on a date.

Finally, always remember that if no one asks, no one gets—in other words, if you don't take the initiative and ask your crush for a date, you're never going to know if the two of you were meant for each other. If you really want to find out if this is the person for you, you're going to have to take the first step—and that first step means doing the asking.

But what if I flub?

"Would I like to go to the movies with you?"

You mean, like that kind of flub? Where you totally screw up the actual question?

That's a tough one. That's definitely embarrassing. And what's worse, the person you're trying to ask out might even laugh in response to a flub like that—and how lame would that be? Maybe you should re-think this date thing altogether, huh?

Don't be ridiculous! Everyone flubs now and then! You're nervous! You like this person a lot and you're asking him or her out for a date—that's a huge step!

I mean, think about the president of the United States for a second. Whenever he gives a speech, he's got a tele-prompter right in front of him, carefully mapping out exactly what he has to say. And even he flubs his speeches some-times! You're doing it on your own, with no teleprompter, and no notes.

If you mess up your "lines" and say something wrong while you're doing the asking, you'll probably feel embarrassed, but the key is not to let it scare you. If your like-object laughs at your mistake, you can laugh along too! And you can even say something like, "Well, that came out wrong. Let me start all over again." Then start again and pretend it never happened. Your like-object will probably be impressed with the way you carried it off.

Whatever you do, don't slink away and act like you just committed a crime. Everyone screws up sometimes—even your crush! Keep your sense of humor and don't beat yourself up for making a natural mistake.

WHAT DO I DO IF HE OR SHE SAYS NO?

The second reason people feel nervous about asking someone out is pretty obvious—they're afraid of the rejection they'll experience if the like-object says "no."

It's never easy to be rejected. It's especially hard if you've just gathered up every last shred of confidence you could muster to ask someone out, and their answer is no. It hurts. You may feel like your whole world has just been shot down the tubes.

Your instincts may be to tell your like-object that he or she is a miserable jerk and you can't imagine what you ever saw in him or her. You've got to keep that under control. Yelling at your (now probably former) like-object isn't going to do any good, and it will make you look like you're a few sandwiches short of a picnic.

It may be a hard thing to do, but if someone says no to you, you've got to keep your confidence level high and keep your act together. Even though you may be feeling lower than a slug, you've got to keep smiling (for a while anyway) and say, "OK. I just wanted to ask. Thanks."

Sounds impossible doesn't it? It's really not. And if you can keep it together for just a little while, you can walk away from your like-object with your dignity intact. You can cry, complain, or insult them once you've gotten home.

When you ask someone out, and they say no, your first instinct will be to think that person doesn't like you. That might not be true! The person may not be allowed to date yet. They might already be dating someone else, someone you didn't know about from another school or town. Or, they might not feel ready to date—they might even be more nervous than you are about it. Finally, they might not have thought of you romantically, like a crush. They might think of you more as a friend, and they might just be totally surprised by the question! And yeah, the truth is they might not like you the way you like them, which stinks, but also isn't the end of the world.

Rejection is hard because it hits you in your self-esteem. You might start thinking there's something wrong with you. You might be thinking, "If I were . . . taller, thinner, blonder, smarter, more athletic, cooler, more popular, or whatever, he or she would have said yes." You might start thinking that there's something about you that you have to change or fix. Coming down hard on yourself is one of the nasty by-products of rejection.

When something like this happens, it's really important to remember your good qualities. Spend time with friends who can support you and remind you about what a good person you are. (Your friends will probably start telling you how much they always hated the person you liked anyway. That always makes people feel better!)

After the rejection, you may feel bad for a while. That's normal. But don't let it overwhelm you—get back into activities that make you feel good about yourself. Slowly, you'll start to forget about the rejection, and the person who rejected you. You'll start to feel confident again—confident enough to ask someone else out when the time is right!

Whatever you do, don't allow one rejection to sour you on the whole dating thing. There are plenty of people who would be happy to go out with you, so don't allow one person's rejection to make you feel like a loser. Just keep those positive thoughts running through your head, and remember there's someone out there who's just right for you. Don't be afraid to keep looking, and keep asking.

It's always a good idea to have a plan, so here are some ways to handle rejection and still keep your pride and dignity intact:

- ✔ *Be polite*—Always say, "Well, thanks anyway" before you walk (never run) away from your like-object.
- ✔ *Keep smiling*—It's tough, but it really helps to keep a smile on your face, even after your like-object has said no. Even if you feel rotten, smile—it takes the sting out of the rejection.
- ✔ *Keep your humor*—This is even tougher, but a light-hearted, "Well, you can't blame me for trying, can you?" before you leave the scene will help ease the moment and give you the opportunity for a clean getaway.

WHAT IF YOU'RE A SHY GUY (OR GIRL)?

If you're a naturally shy person, you might have real problems summoning up the courage to ask someone out—you might have real problems even talking to the person you like! Shyness is nothing to be embarrassed about, but it is something that can limit your social life, so it might be something you want to work on.

The only way to become less shy is to practice. Just try and do a little something every day to help pull yourself out of your shy shell. Start by smiling at people in the hall at school—a warm smile will definitely make you more approachable, and smiling makes you feel better about yourself.

Next, try saying hello to someone new. Set a goal for yourself—promise you'll say hi to at least three new people each day. When you see people responding to you, you'll start to realize that you're a pretty cool person.

Finally, start joining in conversations. It's tough when you're shy—you might feel like you have nothing to contribute, or that your ideas and opinions don't matter. But once you start taking part in chats with people, you'll find that they *are* interested in what you have to say.

And remember—watch your body language. If you tend to stand around with your arms crossed in front of you, or with your head slumped down, you're going to look like you really want to be left alone. Keep your head held high and look people in the eye—let them know you're someone way cool to know.

SOME DATING OPTIONS

When most people hear the word "dating," they think of those romantic one-on-one dates they see in the movies and on TV—you know, where there are always lit candles everywhere. But if that idea scares you a little, you might want to think about some cool alternatives to the traditional dating scene—including making dating a major group activity!

ZAC'S STORY: GETTING REJECTED REALLY HURTS

"I had a part-time job at a fast food restaurant, and that's where I met this girl named Angie—she was my age, but she went to a different school. I really thought she was nice, and we used to talk a lot at work—so one night after work, I asked her out. She said, 'Maybe some time,' which I thought meant yes. But she kept putting me off—with a whole bunch of excuses. Finally, she told me she had a crush on some guy at her school, and she didn't think it was fair to go out with me when she liked him. Getting rejected really hurt my feelings a lot, but what made it worse was that she kind of got my hopes up, then she totally dissed me."

When Your Date is ... Everybody

Group dating is a really new phenomenon—it didn't even exist some years ago. See, you and your friends are part of a totally '90s trend, and you probably didn't even know it!

Group dating also happens to be an excellent way to get your feet wet in the dating game. It's a way to get to know your like-object better, to spend time with him or her in safe surroundings, and in the company of your closest friends.

Actually, the term "group dating" is kind of silly and misleading. You certainly aren't dating everyone in the group, and you're not really on an official "date," because there are so many other people around. But it's an idea that's popular with teens across the country for several reasons:

✔ *It's casual*—There's none of that weird "I'm alone with this person and I don't know what we're going to talk about for three hours" feeling you get when you're on a one-on-one date with someone.

✔ *It's flexible*—You can go to the movies, the mall, or to a sporting event—the only limit to a group date is your imagination.

✔ *It's way fun*—Even if you and your like-object aren't talking and laughing up a storm, you're still hanging out and having a good time with friends. The odds that you'll have a blast are very good.

✔ *It's safe*—This is what your parents probably like best about it. You're with a crowd, which means you can all look out for each other.

✔ *It's inexpensive*—Ever hear the phrase "cheaper by the dozen"? If a bunch of you go to a restaurant, you can all share the bill (you can also share your like-object's French fries), which means the cost to you and your date is lower than it would be if you were out on your own.

ANNA'S STORY:
I REALLY LET IT GET ME DOWN

"The first time I ever asked someone out was a serious horror show! I had a crush on this guy named Rob, and I really wanted to ask him out, so I got up my courage and I asked him one day after school. He laughed and said no way. He told me I 'wasn't his type'! I was so hurt and humiliated by his rejection, I went home and just cried for like, hours. Later I told my best friend about it, and she told me she thought he was a real jerk. We started laughing about it, and I felt better. But when I saw him at school the next day, he avoided me and wouldn't even say hello. I felt hurt all over again. I really let it get me down, and I didn't ask anyone out again for a long time. I also said no to a guy who asked me out because I felt so bad about myself. Looking back, that was really a stupid reaction I had. I mean, it was obvious the guy I liked didn't really like me, so what did it matter if he said hello to me or not? I finally got over it and started acting like myself again. Later that year, I asked out a guy I met at my church group, and we started dating—I really liked him and we had a lot of fun together. Then, wouldn't you know it, one day Rob comes up to me in the hall at school and asks me out to a movie! I couldn't believe it! I told him, 'No way!' He looked really hurt, so I said, 'Maybe next time you won't be so mean when someone asks you out. Maybe you'll think about how that person feels!' Then I turned around and walked away from him."

So how does group dating work? Basically, you, your friends, and everyone's like-objects get together for a group activity—let's say, a night out at the movies, followed by dinner at the local pizza restaurant. Everybody meets in front of the theater, or at someone's house, and then there's a mass convoy to the site of the activity. (If none of you drive yet, you'll have to get some "designated parents" to do the driving—more on that sticky issue in the next chapter!)

What makes this "group dating" rather than just another outing with your friends is that everyone in the group is "paired off"—you and your like-object, your friends and theirs. During the course of the evening (or afternoon, of course) you and your like-object can hang out together, talk, even hold hands (if you're really in like!)—the two of you get the chance to be together, without the pressure and the nerves of a one-on-one date.

Group dating may be something you and your friends will want to try. It definitely has a load of advantages. But, it also has some disadvantages you might want to think about:

- ✔ If your like-object is paying more attention to his or her friends (or, worse yet, if he or she seems to be paying special attention to someone other than YOU), you're going to get seriously ticked off. A dis like that could really hurt your feelings and spoil the day.
- ✔ If you discover you don't really like your like-object as much as you thought, it's a little too easy to dis THEM! You could be the one causing the hurt feelings.
- ✔ Big groups of people can get loud and rowdy—something that might spoil the dating atmosphere you'd hoped for.
- ✔ You're kind of stuck doing what the group wants to do—and it might not be something you particularly enjoy.

If you and your friends do decide to try out group dating, keep in mind that the experience is supposed to be fun. Look at it as a cool way to spend time with your friends, and an excellent way to get close to your crush—without getting too close, too fast.

Double the Fun

The double date is a concept that's ancient—you and a friend, each with a date of your own, go out together. It's fun, and it's almost foolproof. If things get boring, or you discover your date has a hard time putting noun to verb to form a full sentence, you've always got your friend to talk and laugh with.

I said "almost foolproof" for a reason. There are things that can go wrong, things that can actually screw up your friendship even more than your relationship with your date.

For example? If your friend and her date are getting along great, while your date is sticking straws up his nose, you're going to get really agitated. Believe me.

Another example? You and your date are holding hands and smiling at each other while your buddy and his date are fighting like cats and dogs about how much ketchup to put on the French fries.

In both these scenarios, you're most likely to get pissed off —at your friend! Even though your friend hasn't really done anything wrong—other than doing the opposite of what you're doing—you're probably going to resent him or her. In fact, you're going to resent your friend specifically because he/she isn't experiencing what you're experiencing.

So how can you double-date and ensure a great time is had by all? You can't really ensure anything, but you can plan ahead.

Make sure you and your friend understand that both your welfare and your good time are important—but your friendship is more important. If one of you is having a bad time and wants the date to end, the other should agree to end it (of course, if you're having a blast with your date, be sure and let him or her know that—and assure him/her that you want to plan another date soon). Another key to a successful double date is to keep it super casual—do a movie, or head out to the skating rink instead of planning a romantic dinner or a daylong date. And finally, remember that your relationship with your friend is just as, if not more, important as your developing relationship with your date. Don't get angry with your friend just because he or

MY OWN BLINDING EXPERIENCE

My blind date experience happened when I was in tenth grade. An acquaintance of mine told me that someone she knew thought I was cute, and asked me if I'd be interested in going out with him. I was flattered and said yes. She arranged a double date and we all went out to the movies, then to a diner for a snack. My date was very nice, a total gentleman. At least I assume he was a gentleman. The fact is, he didn't say anything to me the entire evening! I mean nothing, other than "Hi" and "Good night." And he had really weird hair—I mean, it was a strange length, a strange color, and a strange style. He sort of looked like those old busts of Beethoven and Mozart you see in museums. It was the longest night of my entire life.

In my opinion, dating is hard enough when you really like the person you're going out with. It's triply hard when you don't know the person you're going out with. And it's twenty times as hard when you're faced with someone you don't know, who looks like Scooby Doo.

If you do agree to a blind date, remember to keep it casual—like the double date, only more so. Don't agree to a blind date if the plans include daylong activities. Do a movie, lunch, or a social activity like skating or bowling. And if the date is a flop, go home.

Hey, you might be one of the lucky ones. You might actually meet the love of your life on a blind date.

But remember, no one knows what you like the way you do—if you do the choosing, you're more likely to select a date who shares your interests, and who doesn't look like a cartoon character.

she is having a better or worse time than you are. Remember that it's just one night or one afternoon—your relationship with your friend should mean more to you.

The Blind Leading the Blind

Some people swear by them; others detest them. Your parents might have met on one, or your mom may still not be able to talk about the one she went on in tenth grade. They're blind dates. And people have very intense feelings about them.

I went out on a blind date once. Once.

A blind date means you're going into it blind—you don't know anything about the person you're going out with, not even what he or she looks like.

Why would you do such a stupid thing? Well, suppose your cousin, whom you love, tells you she knows a guy from her school that would totally float your boat. He's absolutely perfect for you, she says, and she should know—she's your cousin, whom you love.

So you agree to a double date—your cousin and her boyfriend; you and this perfect guy.

And he comes to the door and . . .

. . . he looks like Scooby Doo.

. . . he's wearing something unbelievably weird.

. . . he immediately starts talking about his collection of bugs.

. . . he's got a habit you gag over—like cracking gum, gnawing his nails, or chewing on a rubber band.

So, you kill your cousin. Oh wait, no you don't.

You go out on the double date and . . .

. . . he turns out to be the perfect guy for you—and you think chewing on a rubber band is way cute now.

. . . you have the worst time of your life and you never let your cousin forget it.

Blind dates are a world of extremes, aren't they?

HOW TO SAY YES

Your like-object, the one you've been crushing on big time, finally asks you out on a date. You know your parents won't have a problem with it; you know you're not doing anything Friday night, and you know you want to go.

So you just say, "Yes. I'd love to go out with you!" That one's pretty simple, don't you think?

What makes your cousin, whom you love, choose such a wacko for you anyway? What is she thinking?

Well, other people often see us differently than we see ourselves. They may see qualities we aren't even aware we have. They may not be aware we're not attracted to Scooby Doo. In short, they may know something we don't, something we're surprised to learn about ourselves. Or, they may just be stupid.

HOW TO SAY NO

So what do you do when you're the one who's been asked out? How do you say yes or no?

Saying no to someone who's just asked you for a date is one of the hardest things in the world. Even if you don't particularly like the person who's just asked you.

Lots of people have trouble saying no even when the situation has nothing to do with dating. Girls often have an especially difficult time refusing a request. Everyone has said yes to something that ends up in disaster for just that reason. Your best friend asks to borrow your favorite jacket, and you say yes—and the jacket comes back covered in mustard and smelling like it was used to keep a horse warm. And when your friend asks to borrow your sweater, you say yes just to keep the peace.

It's very hard to say no to someone who likes you, someone who's gotten up the courage to ask you out. Some girls and guys say yes to dates just so they can avoid the discomfort of saying no.

Of course, some people find that the easiest way to say no is to tack a big lie on the end of it. For example, "No, I already have a boyfriend" (when you don't), or "No, my parents won't let me date" (when they will). Too much homework, a sick sibling, or the sniffles are all examples of little white lies you might be thinking of using to get out of an uncomfortable date-asking situation. This may seem like a good option (it's only a little fib after all), but it's actually not saying no—it's postponing the no. If you make up a story to avoid a date, it's possible the person who likes you will ask you out again, and that means you have to make up another lie. And while this might not bother you from a moral point of view, it can get very confusing to keep all your complicated stories straight.

Another lame-o way of saying no goes something like this: "I wouldn't go out with you if you were the last person walking the earth!" This response will get you a great reputation as a real

BRAD'S STORY: ASKING WAS THE HARDEST PART

"My best friend Joey had this cousin who was our age, and I'd met her a couple of times when I was at his house. I really liked her a lot and I thought she was really nice and really pretty. One Saturday, we were all at Joey's house 'cause his family was having a barbecue. I tried to get my courage up to ask her out on a date, and I totally couldn't. I kept practicing what I wanted to say, but every time we were alone, I chickened out. Finally, when everyone was getting ready to leave, I swallowed hard, walked right up to her, and asked her if she wanted to go to the movies with me the next weekend. She smiled this great smile and said yes. We had the best time, and she became my girlfriend. The date part was easy—it was the asking that was hard!"

meanie. Who's going to have the courage to ask you out if you're this nasty?

Then there's always, "I'm not into dating anyone right now." Nice try. But if you start dating someone else the next day, you'll be the cause of some hurt feelings. If you don't, the asker still might ask you out again sometime down the road, when you might be more "into it." It's simply another way to avoid a situation, rather than to deal with it.

So what's the best way to say no to someone you really don't want to go out with? It takes practice to say no with consideration, respect, and compassion, but saying the right thing goes a long way in maintaining friendships and avoiding hurt feelings.

Try this on for size: "I'm really flattered that you want to go out with me, but I really don't think we've got enough in common. Can we just be friends?"

Or how about this? "It was really nice of you to ask, but I really just think of you as a good friend—can we keep it that way?"

Or, if you want to be blunter, you can say, "I'm sorry, but I'm really not interested in going out with you." That might not be the nicest thing to say, but it will get your message across, loud and clear.

Let's face it—no matter how nicely you say no, it's going to bum out the person you say no to. So try to be as nice as you can about it; there's no reason to be nasty to someone who liked you enough to ask you out.

How Are You Gonna Get There?

OK, so if someone's just asked you out, this isn't really your problem. But you might want to keep reading, 'cause you might be asked to help out in this area.

And if you did the asking, congratulations! You are now responsible for taking care of one of the most practical (and pesky) issues in this entire book.

How the heck are we going to get there? This may sound like a silly question, but it's actually a major consideration when you're planning your evening or afternoon (and we'll talk more about "the planning stage" in the next chapter!). It obviously puts limits on where you can go and what you can do. It will also put limits on how one-on-one your date will be.

THE OPTIONS

There are five options when it comes to date-transport. And it doesn't take a rocket scientist to figure out that one of these options is going to be something you're not going to like.

- ✔ You drive
- ✔ Your date drives

✔ You take public trans
✔ You walk, blade, or bike
✔ Your parent or guardian drives

OK, so that last one is really rotten, isn't it? It almost makes you want to cancel the whole thing, doesn't it? Let's go through the first four, and then we can deal with that last one—the one that's making you barf right this minute.

You drive

Obviously, for this to be an option, you have to have a driver's license. In some states, you can get a driver's license (that allows you to drive alone, not a permit, which allows you to drive with an older, more experienced driver) as young as fifteen. In other states (like New Jersey, where I grew up), you have to be seventeen to get your license, sixteen and a half to get your permit.

Your date drives

If you've been asked out by someone old enough to drive, you've finished this chapter and you can jump to the next one.

This scenario was actually the one I experienced on my first date. Matt, the senior who took me out, drove his own car. Well, it wasn't exactly a car. It was a blue Gremlin. It looked like a little kiddie car, but it ran well enough and it got us where we needed to go.

It's very cool and sophisticated to go out with someone who drives. You can also learn a lot about your date by watching his or her driving etiquette. Does he open car doors for you? If you've opened the car door for her, does she lean over and pop up the lock on the driver's door for you? Does he drive well? Is she responsible about the car—keeping it filled with gas, keeping it clean? Are there soda bottles and tons of junk in the back seat? See—a car (and the condition of it) can reveal a whole host of secrets about your date.

Of course, your parents might not like the idea of you dating someone who already drives. They might think the person is too old for you. Or they might think you're planning to get a little physical in the car—something they probably want you to avoid. Or their concern might be purely practical—they may worry about your date drinking and driving, or getting into an accident. These are all rational, reasonable parental concerns.

The best way to deal with this is to remember what you read in an earlier chapter—let your parents meet your date. They'll be able to gauge what kind of person your date is, and with the simple gesture of introducing your date to your parents, you'll be acting responsibly and putting their minds at ease.

You take public trans

This option might seem lame at first glance, but it really isn't the worst option in the world. Some cities and towns have excellent public transportation systems. New York City, for example, has a great subway system, as does Washington, D.C. Many smaller towns have bus service that's terrific—on time and very efficient. Some cities even have trolleys (which are kind of romantic and cool) that can get you around.

REMEMBER . . .

. . . if public trans or a cab is your date transportation choice, and you did the date-asking, YOU PAY FOR THE RIDE FOR YOU AND YOUR DATE! No two ways about it. If you asked your date out, and going out means taking the bus, you pay both fares. Your date may offer to pay his or her share, but if you've got manners, you'll refuse and pay both. It's just the nice, right thing to do.

All of these options cost a little money, but little is the operative word. It's really not a big cost, especially if you think about the importance of getting where you want to go.

If you have a bit more money to spend, you can get a cab to take you from point A to point B. Cabs are everywhere in major cities, but almost every small city and town has a livery cab service. These services cost a lot more than public trans— some one-way rides might be well over $20. But again, if you factor in convenience and peace of mind, it's not much at all.

You walk, blade, or bike

If you've planned carefully, the walking (or roller-blading or biking) option can work for you. In Chapter 11, I list dozens of inexpensive and creative dates—dating choices you can make if you're living on a budget. This list can also help you if you're car-less at the moment.

For example, if you plan a romantic date in a nearby park, you might be able to stroll there. Or, you might roller-blade there, or bike there. Same goes for the beach or lake (if either is close by).

You shouldn't be shy about telling your date that your boots are made for walking. After all, if your date is the same age as you, he or she will understand the bummer-ness of not having a car, and probably won't mind sharing a stroll or a bike ride with you. In fact, you might not have to bring it up at all—it might just be expected. (Bring it up anyway, just to be sure. If your date shows up wearing a dress or dressy pants, you don't want to surprise him or her by pointing out the ten-speed.)

These activities are more than just inexpensive, convenient ways of getting from place to place—they're also fun, healthy ways of getting around. Hey, adults pay good money to get this kind of exercise in a gym!

But even more important, these activities are (or can be, if you're doing them with the right person) very romantic. It's simply nice to walk or bike ride with someone you like. It gives you a good feeling, strolling, or riding your bicycles, or roller-blading with someone special. Don't be shy about suggesting these transport options—they're actually totally cool.

Your parent or guardian drives

Ugh. We hate this so much! I can't even write about it, it's so lame. AHHHH! OK. I'm so over it. Let's get it over with!

Having your parent, guardian, or older sibling drive you and your date to your final date destination probably sounds like the ultimate in humiliation. I mean, how awful is this—you and your date, whom you presumably like a lot, sitting in the back seat while your mom, your dad, or someone else in the family drives you to the ten-plex so you can go to the movies? Gross-out!

The fact is almost everyone has had this "ultimate humiliation" happen to them once or twice in their lives, and everyone gets over it eventually. There's really nothing inherently wrong with having your parents drive you and your date to wherever it is you're going. After all, you don't have a car—your mom, dad, or older sib does. It makes perfect sense that they should drive you, doesn't it?

That is until you think about . . .

. . . how your older sister is going to tease you, and maybe even tell your date about that really horribly embarrassing thing that happened to you in third grade!

. . . how your mom always enjoys singing along to the Barry Manilow tape she keeps in the car for just such occasions.

. . . how your dad picks his teeth with matchbooks, and often goes off on tangents about conspiracy theories.

Yep, your family—they're an embarrassing lot, aren't they?

Again, you're not alone. Everyone gets embarrassed by his/her family now and then. It's really not the end of the world. In fact, your date could probably tell you stories about his or her family that would curl your hair!

Having a family member act as chauffeur is a necessary evil. It's something you may have to do in order to get to your final goal—your first real date. You just really have to keep telling yourself that it's OK and that other teenagers have gone through similar experiences and lived to tell about them.

And you've got to warn your date about the possibility that your dad might start picking those teeth of his. If you've got a good, tight relationship with your parents and siblings, you might want to prep them, too—remind them that this is an important night for you, and that you really want to make a good impression on your date. If this is something you think might make you feel better, then by all means do it.

Unfortunately, in all likelihood, your family will still wind up embarrassing you. And believe it or not, that has more to do with you than them—you're nervous and edgy about your date, and everything they do is going to seem evil. In fact, if they ask you for directions to your date's house you're probably going to go off on them—"What do you mean where does she live? I told you three times already!" (even if you've never mentioned the location of her house before). Little, overly emotional incidents like this one have a way of happening when you're stressed out. And of course, having your mom or dad drive you to your date is probably making you even more stressed out!

The best way to deal with the whole parent driving thing is simply this—relax, be honest about everything (including how you're feeling), and don't make it into a major "thing."

That first one is crucial—relax. Like I told you before, everyone has been through it, and we all lived. In fact, if your date's a really cool person, it might even add to the fun— "embarrassing family" stories make excellent date conversation. You can rehash the car ride and really laugh about it. If your date laughs with you, you know you've found a winner. The key here is, if you're relaxed about it, your date will be, too. If you're a bundle of nerves, your date will pick up on it, and it'll add a truckload of tension to an already tension-filled experience.

Part two of these instructions goes something like this: tell your date that your dad, mom, brother, or sister (or someone else in the family) has to do the driving. Make a joke about it—tell your date that no matter how much you like them, you don't think you want to steal a car and drive without a license. Jail time just isn't what you had planned for your future. Then, be honest with your parents. Tell them you're nervous about them driving, that you're a little embarrassed about it, and although you're sure everything will be just fine, you just thought you'd mention how you're feeling. If your older brother or sister is driving, you might want to bribe them to be quiet about that thing that happened in third grade.

Finally, don't make it all out to be more than it is. Really—in ten years, you're not going to care how you got to the date—you're just going to remember whether or not you had a good time on it.

RACHEL'S STORY: IT REALLY WASN'T THAT BAD

"I was fourteen when I went out on my first date—and the guy was fifteen—and we went to the movies. His dad would be driving us, which seemed to make Jason think I would say forget it! But I said it didn't matter, and on Saturday afternoon Jason and his dad were there to pick me up. I remember Jason was nervous. He barely said a word while we were in the car. His dad talked a mile a minute. When we got to the movie theater, I said, 'Thanks,' to his dad and Jason looked like he wanted to crawl into a hole. It was all he talked about— about how lame his dad was. It was so not a big deal—it really wasn't that bad. I thought it was nice of his dad to do it. I think Jason made it worse by acting that way."

Who's Paying for This, Anyway?

6

Have your parents, or perhaps your grandparents, ever uttered this totally annoying sentence: "When I was your age, things were a lot simpler/easier/better/different." Well, when it comes to money, they're actually right on . . . the money!

You see, when your parents and grandparents went out on dates (which they did, don't let them kid you!) the method of payment *was* simple—the guy paid for everything, from the movie to the meal, from the concert to the ball game. He also paid for the gas in his car and any other incidentals.

Of course, back then it was definitely the guy who did the asking—girls just didn't ask guys out back when your grandparents were young. So it made sense that the boy took care of all the expenses. After all, it was the guy who started the whole process rolling in the first place.

These days, of course, things are a lot more complicated. First of all, these days the girl can be the one who initiates the date, which changes the whole dating dynamic. When the girl does the asking, she actually becomes more responsible for the practical matters surrounding the event.

Secondly, there's group dating, which probably didn't even exist when your grandparents were out and about. Group dating is fun, casual, and cool, but it can be confusing when it comes time to pay the bill at the end of the night—everyone is obviously responsible for tossing some cash into the crew till.

Finally, we're living in a world where the finer, fun things in life get more expensive every day. I myself have seen the price of movies double in my lifetime. Food, movies, concerts—everything costs money, and sometimes an awful lot of it. It often just isn't fair to expect any one person to pick up the check all the time.

And so, guess what? Things *are* different today than they were in your parents' and grandparents' day. They got that one right. Now the trick is to make it all simple again.

WHO PAYS WHEN?

You Ask, You Pay!

There's a very simple rule of thumb you can follow when it comes to paying for dates. Whoever did the asking does the paying.

If you're a guy, and you ask out your favorite girl, you pay for the date. If you're a girl, and you ask your male like-object to the movies, you pay for the date.

It makes sense. Obviously if you hadn't asked, this date wouldn't be happening, so it's clear that the asker is the one who should foot the bill for the evening (or afternoon). This seems obvious—but you'd be surprised.

Don't take this rule of thumb for granted though. Because nothing in the world is guaranteed, it's very important to bring along some emergency money even if you're the person who was asked. It would be pretty embarrassing if you ended up at a restaurant and the guy who made such a fuss about asking you out suddenly couldn't afford to pay for your hamburger. (It's happened to me a bunch of times!) If you've got some emergency cash stashed in your pocket, you can make sure you don't end up washing dishes or waiting tables to pay off your bill. A good rule of thumb—stash between $10 and $30 in your wallet before your leave the house. That will help take care of anything that might go wrong with the financial planning.

Also, even if the person who asked is paying for everything, it's a good rule to pay for something yourself. If the person who asked you out pays for your movie ticket, it's nice to buy the popcorn. If the person who asked is paying for dinner, you can spring for some ice cream for dessert. If the asker pays the price of admission to a roller rink, you can rent both your skates.

Why should you, you might be asking? If someone asked me out, why should *I* have to pay for anything? Because it helps to solve a crucial problem that could arise later—the "you owe me something" problem. (I'll talk more about this in an upcoming chapter.) Some people think that when they pay for a date, they're owed something in return—a kiss goodnight at the very least, sex at the very most. You'd think this wouldn't still be going on in this day and age, but it does. People—most often guys, but girls too!—still seem to view their date investment as a down payment for a little sumptin' sumptin' later that evening. If you throw some of your own money into the mix, you can defuse this problem before it flares up. If you've made a contribution to the date, no one can hold money over your head. No one can say, "I paid for the movie, now you owe me something."

Contributing to the date is also good for your self-esteem. It shows that you're not a passive partner in this dating game. Being able to take care of yourself—and in some ways, of someone else—shows that you're independent and capable.

It also happens to be a nice thing to do. As I mentioned before, going out is definitely not a cheap prospect. I go to the movies a lot, and I know exactly how expensive popcorn and snacks can be—you practically have to mortgage your mountain bike to pay for a soda! Offering to pay for something is simply a considerate move. It shows you're concerned about the person who asked you out.

For a lot of girls (and a lot of girls' parents) the notion of paying for something on a date is totally foreign. I've had girlfriends who wouldn't even lend their dates a quarter for the phone! But I disagree with that mindset entirely. No matter who did the asking, paying for something is a neat way to show how much you care. It also shows off a girl's independence and confidence—it lets the guy know that you're a girl who can take care of herself, and believe me when I tell you, that's a very attractive trait.

Having the guy pay for everything on a date is definitely the more traditional route—it's been done that way for years, and lots of people (especially girls) seem to think it's a system worth keeping. But if the purpose of a date is to enjoy yourself and have a good time with someone you like, does it really matter who does the paying?

Not for the first date, it doesn't. Down the road, if a long-term relationship develops, it will matter more. It's really lame when one person always pays, and the other always enjoys the free ride. (You might even know couples where that inequality already exists, where one person is always shelling out money and the other never spends a dime—it's ugly, isn't it?)

But for your first date, money shouldn't be an overwhelming concern. The important thing is to get out there and have a good time. So we've come full circle; your best bet is to refer to rule number one—whoever does the asking does the paying. And whoever's been asked does the nice thing, and helps toss in for incidentals. It's a good plan!

Split the Difference

The old expression "Dutch Treat" isn't really in vogue anymore—it refers to a date where each person pays half of everything. Again, with prices what they are, splitting a bill is a perfectly logical thing—it definitely takes the pressure off, money-wise.

But splitting bills is honestly something that happens more often when you're already in a relationship. If you've been dating someone for a long time, it makes sense to split bills—you don't want one of you to go broke, do you?

Talking about money is not one of the most romantic things you can do, but when it comes to dating, it's sometimes necessary. If you've been asked out on a date, you can probably assume the asker is going to be paying for it, but if you're not sure, ask. Or, just bring along enough emergency money to cover your end should you find yourself splitting the bill. (Again, $10 to $30 dollars is a good stash—it depends on what you're doing on your date. If you're going to a fancy restaurant, you might want to lean toward the high end of the suggested amount.) If you did the asking, and you're planning on asking your date to split the bill, be sure and mention that to them before you walk into that four-star restaurant.

The Group Rate

Obviously, if you're going out with a big group, the dynamics are different—and unique to each group situation. If you're one of six people, and

JACKIE'S STORY (YES, THIS ONE IS MINE)

"I once went out on a date with someone I thought was very special. He took me to a very expensive restaurant, and I was really impressed. We had a great dinner, but when the check came, he looked really nervous. He excused himself from the table, and when he came back, he told me he didn't have enough money to pay for the meal. And let me tell you, it was a pretty high bill! Luckily, I had just gotten paid the day before, and I still had the envelope with my week's salary in my purse—it just so happened I forgot to deposit it into the bank. I gave him a good portion of it to pay the bill, but I kept wondering what would have happened if I had made the bank deposit?"

DARREN'S STORY: I HAD TO TAKE A BREAK

"I was always taught that if I asked a girl out on a date, I was responsible for paying for the date, and I had no problem with that. But it got to the point where I really had to take a break from dating—it just got too expensive. I mean, I worked an after-school job, and I was trying to save money for college, and I was blowing all my money on dates. So I stopped dating for a while. Then I started getting into going out in a group. That way, everyone kind of split everything down the middle, and it was a lot less expensive. I was just happy to have a social life again. When you're in high school, it's just not possible to be the big spender all the time. You've got to kind of take a step back and realize that you can't pay for everybody's good time— you won't have any money left at all."

you're all doing something together, you'll probably each be responsible for paying your share of the bill. If, however, you're in a group, but paired off with a particular person, things can get a little complicated. Again, use the standard rule—whoever did the asking does the paying.

But what if no one actually did the asking? What if the pairing off was kind of a spur-of-the-moment thing? This is where your emergency money comes in big time. Rather than create some kind of weird "who pays for what?" argument, you can each just take care of your own portion of the bill. You can wait for your first one-on-one date to splurge.

The Proof Is in the Plans!

7

So you've been asked out on a date—or you asked someone out and he or she said yes. Great, fantastic, you're totally excited and totally happy. Now you've got some planning to do. Oops, did I say a dirty word? Planning?

A lot of really cool things happen without any input from the outside world. Flowers bloom, the sun rises and sets, the tides roll in and out—nature takes care of everything, and everything happens naturally.

Your first date is not the sun. It is also not a flower. It is a date. And if you leave things to chance—or even "nature"— you're going to wind up hanging out on a street corner in front of the local dry cleaners watching cars drive by.

Let me say a few words about "hanging out." When I was in high school, hanging out was an accepted form of social interaction. We hung out in the high school parking lot, in the fields up on the hill, and even in front of our local dry cleaners. And we did absolutely nothing—except hang out.

Some people might argue that we talked to each other. This was actually not true. We did chat, but we spent most of the time looking around—waiting to see who else would show up to hang out with us.

Now, there's nothing innately wrong with hanging out. It's just not a date. It's especially not a first date. A first date is supposed to be special, something to remember. And to make it special, it needs to be planned.

WHAT IS A PLAN?

By planning, I do not mean going nuts over the smallest details. I do not mean arranging elaborate events or scheduling things to the last second. I simply mean, planning.

Eventually, each and every one of you reading this book will experience the silliness of the unplanned date. It usually goes something like this:

You and the one you like a lot are sitting on your front steps, or in your living room. One of you says, "What do you want to do?" The other says, "I don't know. What do you want to do?" This goes on for say, an hour, before one of you gets up and says, "Oh this is stupid. Let's just go somewhere!" The other says, "Where?" and the first person sits back down, and the whole thing starts again. A loving couple can go through this process once or twice every weekend—and they usually end up sitting home watching *Terminator* for the seventy-fifth time.

And you know what? If you've been with your loved one for a long time, that's just fine! It's not fine for the first date.

Why? Because when you're going out with someone for the first time, you're both relative strangers—even if you see each other every day at school. You don't know what this person is really, really like. You will want planned activities to help ease you over the uncomfortable silences and nervous moments that will probably occur. You will want to do something, something fun; you will want a place to go, a destination or a goal. You'd be surprised how calming it is to know where you're going and what you're going to be doing.

So you'll need a plan. But remember, your plan doesn't have to be expensive or elaborate. It can be anything you want it to be. Here are some examples:

- ✔ Plan to go to a seven o'clock movie at the ten-plex, then grab a pizza at the restaurant in the mall.
- ✔ Plan to go to the beach, and pack a picnic lunch to bring along.
- ✔ Plan to go out to a nice restaurant—make reservations (if you have to) for seven-thirty.

See, nothing complicated. Nothing outlandish. And nothing written in stone—a plan is just a blueprint. If something changes, you can change your plans accordingly. But having an idea of what you'd like to do on a date is totally important—you'll really like the results!

"SO WHAT DO YOU WANT TO DO?"

When I was a teenager, and I was asked out on a date, I was sometimes asked the following question:

"What would you like to do?" (A variation of this question was "Is there anything in particular you'd like to do on our date?")

My answer was always the same—"Whatever you'd like to do!"

I thought I was being demure, ladylike, feminine, and properly passive—after all, the guy doing the asking was, indeed the guy—he should make all the plans, shouldn't he?

I was not being ladylike or feminine. I was being a big, passive, no-help jerk. When a guy asks a girl "What would you like to do?" he is not just being polite—nine times out of ten, he really wants to know what you want to do. In fact, chances are good that if you told him what you'd like to do, you'd both end up doing it.

In fact, that goes for both guys and girls—if someone asks, "What would you like to do?" they're really curious. They want to know what you would most enjoy doing, what would make you happy, what would make you smile. And if they can, they'd like to plan a date that would do all those things for you. So rather than playing dumb, why not simply answer the question. If there's a movie you'd like to see, mention it. If you've been dying to try out the new batting cages in town, bring it up.

The thing I'm getting at is this—the person who asked you out on the date may ask you if there's something special you'd like to do. He or she is trying to get your input, which will make planning a cool date a lot easier. If you have an idea for something excellent, something fun, or something new, you shouldn't be afraid to suggest it. The person doing the asking will probably be delighted to hear your ideas—and will probably be psyched to include them.

Of course you could take the easy—and wussy—road that I used to take, and just throw the ball back into the asker's court: "Whatever you want to do is fine with me!" That sounds like a really polite answer, but it often is an expression of fear. You're afraid to state your opinion because you don't want to sound pushy.

Of course, you really might not have any opinions about what you might want to do on a date. That, as they say, is a problem for another book.

But chances are, you have plenty of opinions. For example, I've always been a huge movie fan. A movie has always been a perfect date to me. So when someone asked me, "What would you like to do?" I could easily have said, "A movie would be great!"

If you're the date initiator, it's always nice to ask for date suggestions from the person you've asked. If they respond with, "Whatever you'd like to do," then you can take that to mean you're going to be doing the date planning. (If, once you're on

the date, the person you asked out is not enjoying what you've planned, don't stress—remember, you asked!)

LESS IS MORE!

Here's a great date plan: pick your date up in a limo, rush off to a fancy-schmancy five-course meal, followed by a wild concert—where you've got first row seats, of course! Right. And pigs have wings.

Very few of us can afford such indulgent dates, let alone such indulgent *first* dates. Unfortunately, too many people equate a great date with an expensive date. They assume that if the asker spends a ton o' money, then everyone will have a fab time.

The truth is, even if you splurged for a date like the one I described, your like-object might still have a totally terrible time. After all, if you're not a perfect date match, it doesn't matter how much you spend. And what's worse, if you and your date do get along, and go out again, he or she might expect another mind-blowing date—and that could run into a fortune you really don't have.

So while first dates should definitely be special, and carefully planned, they shouldn't be extravagant or ridiculously expensive. Budget your money, figure out what you can spend, and plan accordingly.

But the less-is-more hypothesis has to do with more than money—it also has to do with time. The dating experts agree that a first date should be a relatively short one. It should be long enough for the two of you to get to know each other—to give you time to talk and share your thoughts. It should not, however, involve an eight-hour day.

You might be asking yourself, why? Why wouldn't you want to spend an eight-hour day with someone you like?

If you think about it, it's way simple. Aren't you nervous about this date? Aren't you excited and a little apprehensive, wondering how it will turn out and whether you'll make a "love connection" like they do on TV? Think about being nervous for eight hours! Think about the way your stomach feels when you're around your like-object—do you really want that feeling to last for hours on end?

If you keep your date down to a reasonable amount of time, you can still enjoy the dating benefits—you'll be spending time with someone you like, and you'll be able to get to know them better. And if everything goes well, you can always plan a really amazing second date, when you'll be much more relaxed (as will your like-object!).

KEEP YOUR QUIRKS UNDER CONTROL—FOR NOW

You're the hugest wrestling fan who ever lived—so you're planning to take your date out to a WWF match!

You're so into *Star Trek* it's scary—so you're treating your sweetie to a day at a trekkie convention.

There's no one who loves Meryl Streep more than you do, so for your first date, you're going to take your honey to a double feature of *Sophie's Choice* and *Out of Africa*.

DON'T DO IT!

Look, what you like and who you like are definitely big parts of you. But there's no guarantee your like-object is into the same things—at least not in the same way that you are. That's why I talked so much in Chapter 3 about getting to know your crush and seeing if the two of you have things in common.

But even if you know your like-object is a big supporter of your school's wrestling team, that doesn't mean he or she is into the big body slams. Basically, what I'm saying is this: don't plan long dates (we know that) that involve intense events. Even the biggest *Star Trek* fan might freak out at a

MICHAEL'S STORY: TOO MUCH TOO SOON

"It was my first date with Angie, and I wanted it to be special, so I planned to take her to Disneyland—I mean how fun is that, right? So my dad drives us out there at ten o'clock in the morning, and I tell him to pick us up at around five o'clock. This was like, the biggest mistake in the world. It started off great—we rode the rides and hung out and had fun. But by about one o'clock, right after lunch, she starts getting really, really tired. And there are like, a million people in the park that day, so we're all crowded and hot and tired, and we start getting cranky. By three o'clock, she was yelling at me. I'd say, 'You want to do this?' or 'You want to go here?' and she'd just yell, 'Leave me alone! I just want to sit here and rest!' By the time my dad picked us up, we weren't even talking to each other. I figured she'd never go out with me again, but she did. I realized that spending the whole day together was a case of too much, too soon. I mean, we didn't know each other that well, and when we started getting tired, we didn't really know what to do about it—so she started yelling, and I started feeling bad. But we're still together, and we've been back to Disneyland a bunch of times—it's always great!"

convention—save it for later, when your date tells you she owns her own personal pair of Dr. Spock ears.

You get it—remember, less is more. Don't surprise your date with something unbelievably overwhelming, especially for your first night out. Get to know your date as a person, then break out the hankies and watch all the Meryl you want—together.

The 411 on the Pre-Date

8

So you've planned your date, you know how you're getting there, and you know who's paying—now what? Well, there are plenty of things to keep you busy in what I like to call the "pre-dating hours."

WHAT DID I DO NOW?

You might be noticing something about the person who asked you out on the date (or the person you asked)—he or she isn't talking to you too much, about anything. This is especially true if today is Wednesday, and your date is planned for Friday night. You might even be thinking the person is changing his or her mind, that he/she doesn't like you anymore, or that you did something wrong.

Don't be worried—this is an example of extreme nervousness on both your parts. Even though the two of you obviously like each other (since you both agreed to share this first date experience together), you're both nervous about the upcoming event. You're not sure what to expect and you're probably both anxiety-ridden. The best way to deal with it might seem to be simply not talking about it. But since it's big on both your minds, it's hard to think about anything else—thus, you end up avoiding each other or, at least, avoiding conversation.

Again, don't stress. Unless one of you cancels the date (and you're not planning to do that, are you?) it's still a go, still a done deal. You're still going out together. If nervousness is making you both tongue-tied in class, it's all OK—you'll have more to talk about on Friday, won't you?

SETTING IT IN MOTION

Your main mission during these pre-dating hours is to set the wheels in motion for the perfect date.

The first thing you want to let your date know is what time you're going to pick him or her up. If you've planned the date, this should be a no-brainer—if the movie starts at seven o'clock, for example, you'll want to arrange a pick-up time of about six-thirty (give yourself enough time to get there, buy snacks, and get settled—you don't want to be crawling over people in the dark once the flick has already started). If you're the ask-ee, it's your responsibility to let your date know about any curfews you have, and what time you can be ready—if you've got band practice till four-thirty, you might want to suggest a later pick-up time. This is something you both must arrange together.

Be aware of one very important thing—being late is lame! Never, ever show up late for a date, and always be ready at the agreed pick-up time. Do whatever it takes to get to your date on time—in fact, showing up five minutes early is extra-cool. No one likes to be kept waiting, but that's especially true for a first date. That nervous feeling is just going to get worse if your like-object is sitting at home, chewing his or her nails, waiting for you to show up. (I know whereof I speak; my prom date was forty-five minutes late picking me up—car trouble. Of course he didn't think to call and let me know! By the time he showed up, I looked and felt like the creepy killer in *Scream*.)

Remember, your first impression is major—don't blow it by being late.

Of course, being too early isn't cool either. You don't want to arrive while your date-to-be is still in the shower. Then you'll end up having to make conversation with your like-object's family—not the worst thing in the world, mind you, but not something you really want to do when you're nervous.

Try your best to arrive at your pick-up point five to ten minutes early. That will show your date that you're prompt, thoughtful, and most importantly, looking forward to the date, but that you're not overanxious.

The Gifts That Keep on Giving

In the old, old days of dating, it was totally common for the guy to bring his girl a gift on the first date. These gifts even had names—they were courting presents. A young male suitor wouldn't be caught dead on his lady-fair's doorstep without some token of his affection—some candy, or flowers, or something equally sweet.

These days, bringing courting presents is totally lame, right?

Well, yeah—but it can't hurt!

Guys, if you want to make a super-duper first impression on your first date, bring a little something special. It doesn't have to be five dozen roses—most girls would be thrilled to receive a single rose, or even a small bouquet of hand-picked flowers. Candy is usually a dieting no-no, but what girl wouldn't be psyched to receive one of those gigantic Hershey's Kisses? There's a whole slew of small, inexpensive gifts you might want to bestow on your like-object—little teddy bears or key-chains are always adorable, and you can bet you'll be aces with your date!

For girls, buying a guy something for a first date is a lot tougher. A lot of guys will blush and look uncomfortable if you buy them something "mushy." But there are ways around the mush factor. If your crush likes a certain sports team, you could buy him something with their name and logo on it.

Once you've figured out what you want to buy, just go pick it up, wrap it up, and bring it home. Then keep the gift out so you don't forget to bring it along with you when you go to pick up your date. If you're being picked up, just leave it in an obvious place so you don't forget about it in the rush of preparation. A thoughtful little gift is a great icebreaker—and it really shows that you think your date is someone extra special.

The Curfew Crises

Curfews are a teenager's worst nightmare. Sometimes it seems like everyone in the whole world can stay out later than you can.

Chances are your parents have already laid down the law when it comes to your curfew—you probably already know what time you're expected to be home, and there's probably no chance your 'rents are going to give you an extra hour or two for something as special as a first date. Or will they? Be sure and talk to them sanely and reasonably before date night. Ask them if it's possible to have an extra hour or two, seeing that this is a super-special occasion. It's quite possible they'll give in and let you have a little more time.

Whether they do or don't, it's especially important to let your date know exactly what your curfew is—and stress that you really need to get home in time to make it. Believe me, if you're on a date, and late for your curfew, not only will you be punished, but it's quite likely your parents won't allow you to date your like-object again. Your crush will be crush non grata in your house—he or she will be forever known as the "person who kept you out late."

Be sure to give your date lots of notice about your curfew—don't spring it on him or her the day or night of the date. If you're honest, your date can arrange events and still get you home on time. Your parents will be totally delighted, and you'll have gained a little more of their trust. And remember, chances are your date has a curfew too, and will be happy to know you're in the same boat.

The Family Thing

If you're the one being picked up, chances are it's your family who's going to get to check out your date. When your date rings your doorbell, and you answer, you're going to probably bring him or her in for a second so your family can give him or her the once-over.

While you're screaming with anxiety, I want to make a point—the biggest loser thing in the world would be if you (or your designated driver) pulled up in front of your date's house and honked the horn. I was way lucky 'cause no one ever tried that—lucky because my father once told me if someone honked a horn for me, he'd go out and shove that horn . . . somewhere unpleasant. Most parents have an instinctive hatred for people who honk car horns to get their teenage kid's attention. When I was younger, I didn't really get it, but now I do—car horn honking implies a lack of respect for your family. It means the person doing the honking doesn't think enough of you and your family to park the car, get out, walk up the walk, ring the doorbell and come in to say hello. So here's another simple rule: if you're doing the picking up, go to the door and expect to be invited in. If you're being picked up, let your date know if he or she honks, someone in your family will be doing some painful horn shoving.

OK, back to the family thing. If you're being picked up, let your date know he or she will be expected to come in and meet everybody. It's no big deal really. Remember the "Who's Driving" chapter? Your family is way more embarrassing to you than to anyone else. Even if someone in your family does something silly, chances are your date will be so nervous that he or she won't notice.

Which brings us to the real point—it's the person who's meeting your family who will be the most nervous at the meeting moment. They'll feel like they're being totally studied and scrutinized. Because the thought of meeting your folks scares them, they might try and squirm out of it, saying they'll meet you someplace rather than actually coming to your house.

Don't let that happen! Having your date meet your family is an important step in building trust between you and your folks. Your 'rents will be more likely to trust you if they know you're willing to bring your dates (and all your friends) home. It also lets your date know that you have a family who cares about you, who is concerned for you and excited for you, and who'll be waiting for you when you get back.

Plan Your 'Drobe

Remember what I told you in Chapter 7—no wild surprises on the first date! Here's another good reason to remember that rule: you've got to know where you're going if you're going to dress properly.

If you and your date are heading out to the movies, you really don't need to wear that strapless black dress, do you? If you and your date are going to nosh at a fancy restaurant, you're going to want to leave those ripped jeans at home, aren't you? And if you're planning something physical, like bike riding or roller-blading, you're going to at least want to be wearing sneakers, won't you?

Once you know what you're going to be doing on your date, you can plan your wardrobe accordingly. You can figure out exactly what you want to wear—then change your mind a hundred times. But at least you've got a game plan!

Remember—it may be tempting to get overly dressed up. You might be thinking, hey, if I wear that really hot outfit I bought at the mall last week, I'll really make a great impression on my date! But you'll make a better and bigger impression if you dress properly—and you'll feel more comfortable if you're wearing something that's perfect for the occasion.

Clear the Decks

If you possibly can, clear off your schedule for date night. If you've got chores at home, see if you can switch 'em with your sibs for one night. If you've got something to do after school, try and postpone it. Make sure you give yourself plenty of time to get ready, and don't get distracted by anything. If your friends call while you're getting ready, keep it short—tell them you'll tell them all about it tomorrow. If your little brother is acting like super pest, have your mom lock him in the bathroom. (Not really, but you get the picture?) Give yourself a break if you can—you're nervous, that's for sure, so why not take it easy on date night?

The Waiting Is the Hardest Part

There's no doubt it. Waiting on date night is pure evil!

Use the time wisely. Take a long hot shower or bath to relax you. Do some deep breathing. Write your feelings and your hopes in a journal. Do things that will calm you, and keep you centered and grounded.

LAUREN'S STORY: OH, WHAT I WORE!

"My first date was almost a total disaster! When my crush Jason asked me out, I was so stoked I could have screamed. I went to the mall and bought this really awesome outfit—a black mini skirt, a really cool top, and these way dressy high-heeled black shoes. Anyway, I get all dressed up for the date, and when I open the door, Jason is standing there in jeans and a T-shirt! I'd never asked what we were doing, so I assumed we were going someplace dressy—he'd planned a night at the batting cages! I was so embarrassed, I thought I was going to sink into the floor! But instead, I said, 'Give me five minutes!' and I ran upstairs and changed into jeans while he played a video game with my brother. We both laughed about it later, but it was a good lesson—now I always ask what a date has planned! I saved the awesome outfit for another date!"

HARRY'S STORY: DON'T SWEAT IT

"I was so psyched when Allison agreed to go out with me that I planned this really big-deal date at a nice restaurant. I'm positive I told her that was where we were going—I don't know, maybe I was nervous and forgot. But when I picked her up, she was wearing sweats! Here I was all dressed up in a suit and tie, and she was wearing sweat pants! When I reminded her of where we were going, she said, 'Oh, I guess I'm not really dressed right, huh?' When I told her I didn't think the restaurant would let her in dressed so casually, she said, 'That's just silly. Of course they will.' But I was really embarrassed. I started to think maybe she wasn't as into the date as I was. So I changed plans real quick, and I took her to the diner instead. I never asked her out again, I can tell you that!"

When the Doorbell Rings

OK, your date's here.

You're still nervous, aren't you? You're about to have a screaming fit, right?

Don't stress. Really. It's going to be fine. Just remember, your date is nervous too.

Go for it!

First Date Do's and Don'ts

Once you have all the practical and financial dating issues settled (you know where you're going, you know how you're getting there, and you know who's paying!), you can start worrying about more serious matters—like how do you act, what do you say, and how do you keep from making a complete fool of yourself?

First things first. You should have already told your date that you need to be picked up at your door—no car-horn honking permitted! Make sure your date comes to your door, rings the bell, and comes in and meets your parents. I know, I know—lame! But it will make your life easier in the long run—your date will know your parents are involved and interested in your life and your parents will know your date does not look like a vampire. Or, if he does look like a vampire, your parents will at least know he doesn't bite.

Your parents should also know where you're going and how late you will be. You should have emergency money tucked away. You're as ready as you'll ever be—but you're still nervous. Just walking to the car with your date is making you very, very, VERY nervous.

Never fear! Here's a complete and easy-to-follow guide to a fail-proof first date!

Overdo the manners—Guys, that means open every single door you and your date encounter! Girls, that means you thank him everytime he does it. It means both of you should say please and thank you. It means neither of you should do anything gross—no gum-cracking, no teeth-picking, no disgusting noises. Manners are not old-fashioned and they're not silly—they're the little things you do to show you have respect for the other person.

Don't freak over food—Many dates take place in restaurants, and although restaurants seem like safe places, they are actually way dangerous—they're filled with food that drips and gets stuck in your teeth. But since you're both there to eat, it's totally lame to flip out when the food arrives. If you want to avoid super sloppy meals, go for it—stay away from the spaghetti or the really cheesy pizza, and just say no to anything that includes spinach (for some reason, spinach always finds its way to the space between your front teeth).

If you're going out to eat, EAT—This is something girls are notorious for—you go out to a restaurant with your date, and you order a salad because you don't want him to think you ever eat. Believe me, your date knows you eat—that's probably why he suggested a restaurant to begin with. If you're chomping on rabbit food while he's chowing down on a juicy burger, you're going to look silly, and you're going to be way hungry later on! So girls, take it from me—guys like girls who eat.

Make eye contact—Relationship experts have confirmed that eye contact is the key to building a successful romantic relationship. There is nothing more annoying than talking to your date while he or she is constantly looking into *Deep Space Nine*. Keep steady eye contact with your date whenever either of you is talking. This sincere gesture lets them know you're curious about them, and that you value their conversation and their presence. After all, the two of you wouldn't be on the date if someone didn't say yes—you should be interested enough to at least look at your date. And if you think your date is hot, it shouldn't be that tough, right?

Be honest, about everything—Dates are tough enough without the added pressure of trying to be something you're not. It's always a bad idea to lie about your life. What happens if you go out with this person again? How long will it be until your date finds out you've been fibbing about that 4.0 grade point average or that trophy-case full of football awards? And how will he or she feel about being lied to? Tell the truth—impress your date with your true self! If that doesn't work, find someone else. You'll eventually meet the person who most appreciates the person you really are.

Don't worry about silences—Lots of people freak out when they're with a date and neither person is talking. They think they have to be blabbing every single second of the day—silence equals date failure! NOT! Actually, good quiet moments are signs that you and your date are comfortable together. Let the silences come and go naturally, just like the conversation. You really don't need to be squawking and yakking the whole time you and your date are alone together—use the quiet time to think about what's going on around you.

Don't look at other guys or girls—You're there with your date, and if you really like your date, you shouldn't even notice anyone else in the room. Remember that eye contact, and keep your gaze focused on the person you're with. OK, so you're getting ready to ask me—what if the cutest person in the world walks right past your table? Shouldn't you be allowed to sneak a peek? Don't—it'll make the worst impression possible on your date. If you want to girl or guy watch—hang out with your friends and do it at the mall, not on a date.

Don't talk about exes or former crushes—Don't talk about dates you've had that went bad. You're in the here and now, and you're with your date. Talking about former crushes is boring and hurtful to the person you're with. And if you're with someone who spends all evening talking about his or her exes, don't go out with them again. Chances are, if they're talking about former boyfriends or girlfriends on a first date with you, that's all they're ever going to talk about. And who needs that? And more importantly, who wants to be the subject of this loser's future date conversations?

Keep your sense of humor—If something goes wrong, show your date you have what it takes to roll with the punches. Don't let anything get you down—this is your date, and you're going to have a great time, no matter what happens.

Conversation is the key—If you and your date have nothing to say, the evening will be spent in uncomfortable silence. You may be familiar with the feeling: "What do I say?" "Will I sound stupid if I say something?" "Will I sound too opinionated?" "Too loud?"

When all else fails, ask questions—that's something that will really keep the conversation flowing. Ask about everything—your date's favorite movies, music, or books. You can even ask personal questions. Ask about your date's family, about his classes, about his after-school job—anything you can think of! Hopefully, your date will begin responding with questions for you—that's how real, serious conversations are born!

A red flag if there ever was one—if you start asking questions, and your date starts answering them, that's nice! If your date then starts asking you questions, that's nice too! If you're asking the questions all night, and your date isn't asking you any, it could mean that you've found yourself one self-centered date—definitely uncool. It takes two people to have a conversation. If your date wants to talk to himself or herself, he or she should stay home and talk to the dog.

Another way to get a good conversation started is to talk about the issues of the day! Share your opinions about what's happening in your world. It's a great way to find out just how much you and your date have in common, and it's an excellent way to determine if you and your date share values and principles about all the important things going on around the globe—or at least around the school! Talk about what you're learning in class, or about what you read in the newspaper last week. See if your date is knowledgeable about current issues.

One thing you want to avoid is spilling your whole life story on your first date. That's a sure-fire way to get your date on a fast train away from you! Getting to know each other is one of the coolest things about dating, and doing it slowly is definitely the way to go. If you've got an urge to tell your date about the first tooth you lost, or how you cried on the first day of kindergarten, squash it—at least for the moment. If you like each other and have future dates, you'll have plenty of time to tell your like-objects all your life stories.

Turn off your cell phone—This is something I didn't have to worry about when I was younger—I dated in the dark ages, when the whole world wasn't yakking on cell phones. If you've got one, leave it at home, or at least turn it off. Nothing spells "loser" more than someone who answers a cell phone call on a date, then spends twenty minutes chatting while their like-object is trying to politely not listen in to the conversation.

But wait, you might be thinking, won't my date think I'm cool if I have a cell phone? Won't my date think I'm a person in demand if I'm constantly getting phone calls or pages. NO! Your date will think you're an inconsiderate dork.

Don't be a gossip—OK, so you're still worried about that conversation thing. Why not tell your date everything you heard about that really snotty girl in your economics class—every last down and dirty word? If you want to make a lousy impression on your date, go ahead. Gossiping is totally unattractive behavior, period, but gossiping on a date is just plain boring—and it'll make you look like a nasty, unappealing person.

Share your positive feelings—How gross is it to spend time with someone who never lets you know if they're having a good time? Very gross. Well don't forget, that feeling runs both ways!

LEXY'S FIRST DATE: LAUGHTER MAKES IT ALL OK

"I was out on my first date with this guy I really liked—his name was John and he was in my English class. When he asked me out to dinner, I nearly flipped! We went to this really nice Italian restaurant, ordered dinner, and talked—we were having a great time. Anyway, the food comes, and I start eating my spaghetti, and I drop a huge glob of sauce right on my white blouse! I was so embarrassed, I wanted to crawl under the table! So I looked up at John, took a deep breath and said, 'I think it looks pretty cool! I bet someone would pay a lot of money to own a blouse with such an artistic glob of sauce on it!' He started laughing, and so did I. It really made me feel better, and later, he told me I had a really cool sense of humor."

Let your date know that you're enjoying yourself. If you're having a good time, say so! If your date chose a great restaurant or an especially good movie, give props where props are due. Reinforce your date's self-esteem by giving compliments—and watch your date sparkle with happiness over your praise.

Keep your negative feelings under wraps—OK, so this definitely goes against the "be honest" rule, I admit it. But it's OK to grin and bear it sometimes. If you're bored out of your mind, or you hate the restaurant, or the movie totally bites, you don't have to say so right then and there. You don't have to start screaming about how awful everything is—you can smile politely and get through the evening with your dignity intact. (Just remember the experience, so you know better next time. And remember, if this is what your like-object chose for your first date, the second date can only get worse!)

If you really like your date, but you hate where he or she took you, you can be honest about it—but wait till the end of the date to mention it. For example, if your crush took you bowling (something you really don't enjoy) say something like, "You know, I'm really not the world's biggest bowling fan. Maybe next time we can go play some mini-golf!" This lets your date know you're really into him or her, it's just the activity you weren't thrilled with. It will also be really helpful to your date—he or she will have a better idea of what you like, which will make planning the next date a lot easier.

Don't turn your date into a night at the beauty salon—If you're at dinner, a movie, or a party—whatever and wherever—keep your comb, brush, or make-up hidden away. Nothing is grosser than seeing someone pull out a brush and start fixing the coif at the dinner table. And for girls, that goes double for the make-up—if you want to freshen up your face after eating, take a quick run into the ladies and apply your make-up there. Here's an easy way to remember this tip—if what you're about to do is something you would normally do in the privacy of your bedroom or bathroom, don't do it in public!

When your date is ready to leave, leave with him or her—This sounds like a simple rule, but you'd be surprised how many people think it's OK to say to your date, "Oh, but I'm having such a good time! You go ahead, I'll catch a ride home with someone!"

If your date took you to a party, and you're having a really excellent time, it may seem lame to leave when

JOEY'S FIRST DATE: LOSER WITH A CAPITAL "L"

"I had a crush on this really cute girl in school, and my friends convinced me to ask her out on a date. I was really surprised when she said yes. We went to the movies, which was fine, and then we went out to eat. While we were eating, I realized that she was a total loser—she didn't listen to a word I said, she kept talking about herself, her friends, her classes. She didn't seem the least bit interested in a word I had to say. When I told my friends about it the next day, they all laughed—they all knew she was a self-centered jerk, but they wanted me to find out for myself, so I would get over her."

everyone else is dancing up a storm. But the point of a date is to be with your date—and that means the two of you leave together. Simply say goodnight to your friends and head home with the one that brung ya.

Don't assume that a first date equals a serious relationship—For example, if you run into someone you know while you're out together, and you introduce your date, don't refer to him or her as "my boyfriend" or "my girlfriend." Again, there's plenty of time for a great relationship to develop, but this is a date, not a promise of forever.

Your First Date Checklist

Ok, so now you're a dating know-it-all, and you're ready to go! In fact, your date is going to arrive in about two hours!

Remember, I'm with you here—I want you to have a great time, and to totally enjoy yourself. Before the doorbell rings and your date arrives, why not just go over this handy checklist one more time?

Give yourself enough time to get ready—There's nothing worse than rushing around at the last minute, looking for your lucky quarter, or that skirt you bought especially for the date. Here's a trick—lay out your clothes in advance. Choose your top, your bottom, your shoes, and your accessories, and lay them all out on the bed so you can see how it all looks together. It's a great way to catch any last-minute fashion gaffes. For the girls, if you're wearing stockings or pantyhose, triple-check them to make sure they're run-free. Guys, if you're wearing a tie, make sure it matches the rest of your outfit. Everybody, be on the lookout for stains—remember, you're trying to make an excellent first impression. You don't have to have the most expensive clothes in the word to look neat and clean. And believe me, neat and clean have it hands down over expensive and filthy.

Be on time—Nothing makes a lamer impression than showing up late for your first date! And that thing about being fashionably late—only royal people and celebrities can get away with that! If you're not a member of the monarchy or a cast member on a WB show, get there on time.

Get yourself together—Take a hot shower or a long, relaxing bubble bath before your date—it'll get you clean and calm you down at the same time. Make sure your hair is combed and styled and—DON'T FORGET THIS ONE!—your teeth are brushed! Can you imagine the face your date will make if you smile and reveal a huge piece of GLOP between your front teeth? Gross to the max!

Dress for the occasion—If you know you're going to the movies, don't wear formalwear. If you're going out to a nice restaurant, lose the sneakers and the jeans. But try to avoid "putting on a show"—don't wear anything outrageous (and for the girls, don't wear anything too tight or revealing). Don't buy a new outfit that's completely out of whack with your personality—if you're a girl who normally wears jeans all the time, you can probably find a nice pair of pants and a dressy blouse to wear on a date. You don't have to buy a skintight leopard-print dress for the occasion. You want your date to feel comfortable with you, which means you've got to be comfortable with you.

Prep the family—If you absolutely do not want your little brother in the living room when your date arrives, be sure to let the family know he should be kept on a leash (your brother, not your date!). My dad used to have an issue with wearing shoes around the house, so five minutes before a date was due to pick me up, I'd plop a pair of slippers on his bare feet and run through the house screaming, "Just wear them for five minutes! Five minutes won't kill you!" This calmed everyone down a great deal—not.

Take some time for yourself—If you have time, take a long, relaxing bath or shower to relax you. If you don't, sneak in five minutes of deep breathing or meditating to keep yourself from hyperventilating.

To the girls: Make sure you've gone easy on the make-up—There's something really scary about greeting a date who's wearing seventeen pounds of make-up and another eighteen pounds of lipstick. Keep it clean, natural, and simple. And go even easier on the perfume—he really doesn't need to smell you a mile away.

To the guys: Don't overdo the cologne—If you've showered and washed your hair, you should smell fine, so don't overwhelm your date with huge handfuls of Eternity or Jovan Musk.

Fifteen minutes before the pick-up

Double-check the way you look—If anything is making you feel self-conscious—you don't really love the way the shoes look with the pants, you're not liking that top at all—do a quick change. But don't go crazy and start changing everything, or you'll end up looking like you just trashed a flea market—stick to the style and level of "dress-up" you've already decided on.

Give a mini-fashion show for someone in the family—you'll feel better if someone else confirms how cool you look.

Make sure you have money—If you did the asking, make sure you have

ELAINE'S DATING TIP: BE PREPARED

"I know I sound like a Boy Scout, but when it comes to dates, I believe in being totally prepared. An hour or so before my date arrives to pick me up, I lay out the clothes I want to wear, and make sure nothing is stained or ratty looking. I check my purse and make sure I have everything I'm going to need. When that's all taken care of, I have plenty of time to get myself ready. I don't have to worry about racing around my room, making sure my shoes match my skirt."

CHRIS'S DATING TIP: CHECK IT OUT

"My friends always tease me about the way I dress—I'm always wearing old grungy flannel shirts and ripped jeans to school, things like that. When I go out on a date with someone special, I want to make sure I look really nice, so those flannel shirts definitely stay in the closet. But when I put on nice clothes, I always think I look like a dork. The first time I got dressed up, I asked my sister how I looked, and she laughed at me! But when she saw I was serious, and that I really wanted her opinion, she stopped laughing and started helping me out. Now, when I'm going out on a date, I always check myself out with my sister—she'll always tell me if everything matches, and if I look cool or not."

enough money to cover the date; if you're the ask-ee, bring some emergency money, just in case. You'll feel more confident if you have your own funds in your pocket.

When the doorbell rings

Give yourself one last "once over" in the mirror—Make sure there's nothing in your teeth.

Put on a huge smile and answer the door—Your date has arrived!

Bring your date in to meet the family—I know, this is one of those Maalox moments. It'll be fine—just keep it quick and casual. Don't make matters worse by rolling your eyes or saying something insulting about your kid sister.

Head on out the door—and enjoy yourself!

Dating with Confidence

Dating on a Budget

11

Everyone dreams of that extra-special, romantic, totally outrageous date—the kind of dates you see on TV and in the movies. A romantic, candlelit dinner in a restaurant that overlooks the beach; a ride in a horse-drawn carriage; a trip to an exotic location—those are the magical dating moments you see on the silver screen. Real life kind of stinks in comparison, doesn't it?

Of course, you know that most people don't go out on really extravagant first dates. In fact, most people don't go out on extravagant dates, PERIOD! And most people don't miss it one bit!

THE BEAUTY OF CHEAP DATES!

Sounds pretty awful doesn't it? Cheap dates! What a horrible thought! What type of person would ever take *you* out on a cheap date? You would certainly *never* subject anyone to a cheap date!

Take a chill pill.

The truth is, most young people don't have a lot of spare cash lying around (hey, neither do a lot of adults!) and getting together enough money to treat someone to a really outrageous date isn't always easy. And a person who demands an expensive date when their like-object can't afford one is totally classless!

More importantly, an inexpensive, but special date can be an absolutely beautiful experience. A person who takes the time to think up an interesting, fun, inventive, and inexpensive way to spend time together is a person who really thinks the world of you.

In the long run, a date doesn't have to cost a fortune to be wonderful. Many people will tell you that their most memorable dates didn't cost a single penny—it was spending time with that special person that really mattered.

CHEAP THRILLS!

Here's a sample of some of the great ways you and that special someone can spend quality time together without spending a fortune. And I bet you can come up with a slew of your own ideas, if you really take the time to think about it.

The Park

The perfect setting for a plethora of cool dates, your local park is the place to be anytime of year! Go to your local City Hall or Chamber of Commerce to check out any park activities that might be taking place during the year—many parks have free concerts during the summer, for example. If you're not into a City Hall visit, just read your local newspaper—you'll probably spot announcements for upcoming events. But even if there's nothing special going on, you can turn your town park into the perfect set for some very romantic, fun, and completely cost-free dates.

Total freebies
Roller Blade

Whether you're a beginner or an expert blader, skating around the park is an excellent way to spend a Saturday afternoon—it's physical, so you're getting some exercise, but you can set a slower pace, so the two of you can talk as you skate around the lake. Just be sure to wear your protective gear, no matter how dorky you think you look—you'll seem a whole lot dorkier if you fall and gash open your knee, or worse still, break your wrist.

Walk

There's nothing more romantic than a quiet walk around a lake. The two of you will have a chance to chat and really get to know each other as you stroll. If there's a lake, be sure and bring some breadcrumbs for the ducks.

Bicycle

A great way to get active and share a majorly romantic day—grab your bike and go for a leisurely ride. If you're feeling extra-romantic, you can even grab your date's hand as you glide around the lake.

Play

OK, so you might look totally silly on a swing set, a slide, or a seesaw, but there's no better way to break the ice with someone new than to get really ridiculous on the kiddie rides. More importantly, you'll see if your like-object has a sense of humor—anyone

VOLUNTEER TO DATE

Find out if your special someone has a social-con-science—volunteer your time (and theirs!) at your local animal shelter, your local homeless shelter (you can help serve dinners around holiday time), or at a community center. You can spend quality time together as you help make the world a better place! If your like-object says no, you might want to re-think the relationship—it's impor-tant to share principles and ideals, and if you don't it probably won't last long!

For information on volun-teering (with a date or on your own) check out the Web—just do a search using the word "volunteer" and you'll find a slew of great opportunities to do some good for your com-munity.

who says "I'm too cool to ride a swing" is probably a long-run loser.

Another cool way to play in the park is to wrap up a bunch of board games, cards, and hackey sacks, find a shady tree, and play games all day! Or, buy some beanbags and learn to juggle.

Sing, sway, and dance

Lots of parks sponsor free summertime concerts, and there's nothing nicer than sitting on a blanket, listening to music, and looking up at the stars. But don't be a blanket-potato—grab your partner and dance.

$10 or less
Row your boat

Rent a rowboat and take your like-object for a leisurely row across the lake. Be sure and take turns rowing so one of you doesn't get too tired out.

Eat out . . . way out!

Want to make an awesome impression on your date? Prepare a picnic lunch and share it under a tree in the park! All you need is a basket, a blanket, and some imagination! Make sandwiches, pack up some juice boxes, and sneak in some chocolate chip cookies for dessert. Be sure and bring along a radio or tape/CD player so you can listen to some tunes while you munch lunch.

The Beach
If you're lucky enough to live near the ocean, why not take advantage of the white sand and the cool surf? Most people consider beach dates to be ultra-romantic.

CHEAP DATE CHEERS

Cassanna's Story

"It was my first boyfriend, and I was in ninth grade. We went to this park, and I remember he climbed through the bushes to pick me a rose—and it had thorns on it, so he got scratched! We had a picnic—it was just sandwiches and stuff like that. It was really memorable. I still have the rose—I saved it by pressing it in a book."

Ruben's Story

"I really liked this girl in my class, and so I asked her out, and she said yes. I didn't have a lot of money, so I used a little ingenuity. I picked her up and presented her with a single rose, then we went to the park and watched a little league baseball game. When the date was over, I gave her a coupon that said, 'Good For One Dinner Date—as soon as I get my next paycheck!' She thought that was really funny, and she'd had such a good time at the park, she definitely wanted to go out again! Two weeks later, I took her to dinner at a nice restaurant."

Christina's Story

"On my first date with my first boyfriend we went to see the Christmas tree lighting ceremony in Rockefeller Center in New York City. For some reason, maybe because it was my very first date—I never forgot it. It was really cold, and we were all bundled up, and the Christmas lights were so beautiful. It was magical."

Total freebie

Stroll the boardwalk

Whether it's a mass of rides, attractions and weirdness, or a quiet, peaceful oasis, a boardwalk is always most excellent. If the boardwalk is over-stimulating—games, bells, and lights galore—you can stop, look, and comment on all the wild goings-on; if it's peaceful, you can take advantage of the quiet and have a real conversation with your sweetie.

$10 or less

Hit the beach—obviously!

For a small entrance fee, all that super sand and surf can be yours! (Some beaches do NOT charge entrance fees, and thus belong under Total Freebies, but when you're from New Jersey, you gotta pay to play!) Swimming and splashing in the ocean are a lot of fun, but don't forget to:

- ✔ *Build a sandcastle*—Indulge in your medieval imagination and create a sand masterpiece.
- ✔ *Collect shells*—You'll have a great time examining the gorgeous, pearly shells, and you can take one home for a free souvenir!
- ✔ *Play some volleyball*—Most beaches have nets already set up. Form a team, or challenge your date to a fierce game of one-on-one.
- ✔ *Go surfing*—If you're both into surfing, spend the day hitting the waves.
- ✔ *Put suntan lotion on one another*—This may sound cheesy, but hey, you gotta protect your skin, and who better to apply it than your like-object! (And yeah, I know—it's a great way to get close, too!)

Picnic

Many beaches will allow you to bring your own food and beverages, so pack a cooler with snacks, sandwiches, bottled water, and juice and share a romantic picnic right there on your beach blanket.

Avoid like the Plague

Boardwalk Attractions! Unless you've got an unlimited supply of funds, don't go overboard on the boardwalk. Arcades, rides, and games can be a lot of fun, but they can definitely drain your pocket, and fast! Unless you've got the extra cash to spare, you might want to stay away.

Boardwalk Food! You ever notice how a $1.50 cheeseburger costs $3.50 on the boardwalk? Save yourself some money and bring your own eats.

Other Watering Holes

If you're far away from the ocean, you may still be able to have a wild and wet time. Are you near a lake or a swimming hole? How about a brook or a stream? Any body of water can make a perfect setting for a most excellent date.

Total freebies
Fishing

If you think fishing is just for the fossil set, think again—there's something seriously peaceful and Zen-like about sitting at the edge of a lake with a fishing line cast out. Borrow the family fishing gear, load up on bait and tackle, pack a picnic lunch, and head to your favorite fishing spot. You can talk and laugh as you wait for the big ones to bite.

Walk at the water's edge

Lose the shoes and stroll at the edge of the water. You can have a great time splashing around.

Around Town

No matter where you live, there are plenty of low-cost activities for the two of you to enjoy.

$10 or less

Museums

Think all that educational stuff is boring? Then you've never strolled through a museum with someone special. Walk through an art museum and gaze at the paintings; check out historical homes or villages and learn how people your age lived hundreds of years ago. Take your time and really read those little cards and plaques—it's definitely not dull, and you'll have lots to talk about when you're done.

Cafes

Most cafes and coffee shops don't mind if you sit back, relax, and people watch as you sip your frozen lattes. An added plus—they're air-conditioned in the summer and super-warm and cozy in the winter.

Flea markets and garage sales

Sound lame? Don't knock it till you try it! Walking through aisles of old stuff (antiques or junk!) can be a blast. And if either of you are interested in old record albums, baseball cards, comic books, or music memorabilia, you just might find a hidden treasure.

Zoos

To bring out the animal in you, why not head out to the zoo? Most major cities have huge zoos (some are called conservatories), but small towns often have little petting zoos, aviaries, or other animal habitats available. Why not check out how the animal-half lives?

Fairs and festivals

When the weather gets warm, every city, town, and borough in the country offers a variety of fairs and festivals. For a guaranteed romantic moment, be sure and ride the ferris wheel (how cool to get stuck on top?) and the haunted house. (When

CHEAP DATE JEERS

Dana's Story

"There was this concert in the park, and I went with my crush and a big group of people from school. There was an admission price, but it was really low—less then $5 per person. My crush and his friends insisted on sneaking in, and it was so embarrassing. We had to climb down this steep incline to get to the area, and I fell down and ripped my skirt. And there were all these bugs! But the worst part was, when we got to the concert area, there were only like five people there, so when we all appeared, everyone knew we crashed. There were twenty-five of us, and we had no money—it was like, hi, we're here!"

Ray's Story

"My first girlfriend was really into going out to fancy places, like expensive restaurants. One time, when I was a little short of money, I put together a picnic basket and took her to the park. She complained the whole time, and she broke up with me the next day because she said I didn't treat her right! I found out later that lots of girls think picnics are pretty romantic—and those are the kind of girls I really like!"

Jennifer's Story

"The guy I liked asked me to go to the movies with him, and I was really excited about it. I thought about it for a week, and planned what to wear and everything. But when we got there, he told me he didn't have any money to pay for the movie, and he wanted to sneak in! Normally I wouldn't do anything like that, but I really wanted to have this date with him, so I did, and of course we got caught. The theater manager called our parents and I was so grounded! The thing was, if he had told me he was short of money, I definitely would have treated. As you can imagine, we never went out again—he was bad luck!"

you spot something scary, you've got a perfect excuse to grab your date's hand!)

Bookstores and libraries

Most bookstores and libraries offer readings, which will mentally stimulate you and give you plenty to think and talk about.

The bowling alley

Bowling is a fun physical activity that almost everyone enjoys—even if you're not great at it, you can still have a blast. In fact, if you're both really bad, you'll probably have an even better time cracking up over every gutterball.

The pool parlor

Pool is an awesomely cool activity, and just about every city, no matter the size, has a place to hang out and play.

When all else fails—take a walk

Explore new neighborhoods, visit new stores, and check out the architecture. Or if you have access to transportation, take a ride out of town and go for a nature walk or a long, intense hike. You can chat as you hike, taking in the beauty of nature and enjoying each other's company in really beautiful (and romantic!) surroundings. (One word of caution—if your date suggests a nature hike, and you've got a phobia about critters that crawl, let him or her know and put a kibosh on the idea. Let's face it—not everyone is cut out for everything, and if you freak out over the sight of a snake or a spider, you might feel more comfortable indoors.)

At Home

All right, so hanging around the house isn't exactly your idea of an exciting date. But if it's raining, or you've got to baby-sit your kid brother, you can still have a neat and nice

time with the one you like. And your parents probably won't mind one bit!

$10 or under

Themed movie parties

Rent your favorite movies and create a theme—like disaster movie day, *Godfather* day, or Jim Carrey day. Dress up as your favorite character from the film and see how many lines you can quote.

Kitchen magicians

If your mom doesn't mind, take the date into the kitchen. And do what, you might ask? Mix fruity smoothie drinks in the blender, pop popcorn on the stove, or bake some brownies. But please be sure and clean up, or you may find yourself in the doghouse!

Move to the front

If you've got a front porch or a front stoop (and a warm day!), you've got a great date setting. Sit out front and watch the world (and the cars) pass by. Sip soda, play a game of cards, or just talk. And when the weather gets really, really hot—turn on the sprinklers and run through them until you're soaking wet.

Pet Project

If either of you have a dog, you've got a date! Grab your pooch, hook on a leash, and go for a really long walk. It's a great way to spend time together, and you can bet Rover will add some fun to the afternoon too.

Stormy Weather

Neither rain nor snow nor sleet should stop you from having a great time on a date (well, sleet can sometimes really put a damper on things—but you get the point). Here are some ideas for having a blast when the weather gets nasty.

Let it snow

If you live in a climate where it snows a lot, you're definitely lucky—there are plenty of cool (cold?) and inexpensive ways to have fun!

Total freebies

Build a snowman—It was fun when you were a kid, and it can be even more fun now, 'cause you're better at it! See how artistic you can get!

Have a snowball fight—Just make sure you don't get stupid and start hurling those things at 100 miles an hour—that can hurt, and hurt is something you don't want to get on a date.

Make snow angels—It may sound cheesy, but it's a great way to get silly, and nothing's nicer than warming up inside with some hot chocolate afterwards.

When the rain comes

If you think a rainy afternoon means a dark, dismal, or dreary day, just share it with someone you like.

Total freebies

Take a long walk sharing an umbrella. You can talk quietly and get close.

BREAKING THE BANK

By now you probably can see that having a good time isn't a matter of how much money you spend. All you need is a little imagination, and the person you like, and BINGO, you've got a great date. But if you want to dig into your (or your parents'!) pockets and really spend a wad of cash on your honey, well, you can do that too. Here are some ideas:

- ✔ *Amusement parks*—Totally outrageous entrance fees, overpriced burgers, and souvenirs only Bill Gates can afford—sounds pretty attractive, huh? Still, as a special treat once in a while, an amusement park offers a whole day of fun, wild rides, and awesome adventures.
- ✔ *Sporting events*—If you live near a major league stadium, you can treat your date to a day at the ballpark, cheering on your favorite team, eating hot dogs, and waving those really annoying banners! Just remember that everything is more expensive at the stadium—from the tickets to the soda pop.
- ✔ *Skiing and snow-boarding*—In some parts of the country, the snow-capped mountain is king, and if there's one thing teenagers love, it's braving the elements and going to "extremes." Both activities require equipment and heavy fees, so it's not something you'd want to do on your very first date, but if you and the one you like are into serious snow, a day on the slopes is an awesome adventure.
- ✔ *Horseback riding*—If you live near stables and riding paths, you've got the makings for one of the most romantic, rustic dates. It's not cheap though—most stables charge by the hour, with a one-hour minimum.
- ✔ *Concerts*—Whether you're into pop, rock, jazz, country, or classical, there's a concert out there for you and your date to enjoy. Remember you have to buy tickets in advance—sometimes months in advance, if the featured act is popular.
- ✔ *Under-age dance clubs*—These clubs are an excellent way for young people to hang out, dance, and have fun in a safe and (usually) well-supervised environment. Just keep in mind the entrance fees can be steep, as can the cost of refreshments.

If you think about it, you can probably come up with a slew of high-cost dates, guaranteed to zap your weekly paycheck in one night. As you already know, it's not mandatory that you spend every cent you have on one night out. If your date likes you, he or she will want to spend time with you, not watch you toss your hard-earned money away. But if you want to splurge, there are plenty of opportunities to do so.

When the Date's Over

Eventually, all good things come to an end. And so it will be for your first date. After all that planning and worrying, it will eventually be your curfew time, and you'll have to go home.

Now what?

Ending a date can be the hardest part of the whole dating experience. If you've had a great time, you probably want it to go on forever. If you had a rotten time, you want to go home right now.

When you're getting close to the time you need to be home, remind your date about your curfew. Stress that you've been having a wonderful time, but that you should probably be getting home.

It's always a letdown when a great date comes to an end, but don't let it get you too down—because the best part of the date may be yet to come!

SO WHAT ABOUT THAT GOODNIGHT KISS?

The first goodnight kiss is usually the climax to the first date—and it's totally normal to be stressing out about it. First of all, it's never 100 percent clear if you're actually going to do it; you may be wondering, "Does this person still like me?" "Did I do something to totally screw up?" "Is he still thinking about that popcorn I had stuck in my teeth?" There are probably a million thoughts flying through your mind, all leading to one big worry: Is my date going to kiss me goodnight?

Of course, if your date went badly, you might not even want the person to kiss you goodnight! In fact, there's a possibility that you might be thinking thoughts like, "Wow, she really turned out to be a loser. I hope she *doesn't* try to kiss me!"

The really cool thing about goodnight kisses is they always tend to happen very naturally. If you've both had an excellent time on the date, it's very likely that you'll both want to end it with a wonderful expression of your affection—and that's where the kiss comes in!

Whatever you do, do not leap on your date! Even if your date is a total hottie, and you've been waiting all year to lay one on him or her, don't jump the gun—and don't jump on your date. It's scary and it makes you look like a stalker-type.

When your date is over, her or she will (hopefully) walk you to your door. (Walking your date to the door is right up there with ringing the doorbell rather than honking a horn—it's a respectful thing to do.) If you're with a group, or if a family member is driving you, the logistics of the goodnight kiss may be harder—it's rough to be romantic when you've got an audience. But don't worry—there's usually a moment at the end of a date where you'll find yourselves alone for a few minutes, and that's when the goodnight smooch will probably occur.

I wish I could be specific about the whole kissing thing, but honestly, each date has its own momentum to it. There's no one big moment when the kiss is definitely going to happen. But you'll know when it's about to—there's no way to mistake the signs.

Your date will move a little closer to you and probably tell you that he or she had a great time. Your date might hold your hand or put an arm around you for a little hug.

If you want your date to kiss you, this will be the moment when you'll want to make it apparent. The best way to let your date know you want to be kissed is to tilt your head slightly. This will put you in a perfect kissing position, and it will send out a clear signal that it's all right for your date to lean in and kiss you.

A word of advice: every kiss is different, and everyone kisses in his or her own special way. I remember my girlfriends telling me about French or open-mouthed kissing when I was young, and I thought it sounded a little gross (it's not, but it sounds like it should be!). Your date may kiss you with an open or closed mouth; or your date may give you a less sloppy smooch. But as the song says, "a kiss is still a kiss." Don't start comparing and contrasting your goodnight kiss with the ones your friends have been telling you about. Every kiss is nice, and yours will be extra-nice because it happened between you and the one you like.

Kissing is a natural human instinct, and once you start you won't have to worry about whether you're "doing it right."

Another thing you want to watch for—don't grope your date like they're a cantaloupe! Let your hand rest on your date's arm or shoulder. Remember, this is your first goodnight kiss— you're not kneading a loaf of bread!

When your kiss is over, you can smile and thank your date for the very special evening (or afternoon). One of you may say, "I'd like to do this again" or "Maybe we can get together again soon," but if nothing is said about another date right this second, don't worry about it. (More on that in just a second.)

And that's the end of your first date! Now that wasn't too hard, was it?

"I'd Rather Kiss My Pet Ferret Than Kiss You"

If you're feeling this way about your date, chances are you had a really lousy time. Don't stress—not every first date is the kind you read about in romance novels. Sometimes, a first date goes badly. It just means that you and your (now former) like-object are not meant for each other. You don't have to ever go out with them again if you don't want to. Of course that might leave you with a little problem—what if this cheeseball wants to kiss you goodnight.

Remember how easy it was to let your date know you wanted to be kissed? You just tilted your head! Well, if you don't want to be kissed, there's some clear body language you can use to let them know. After you thank them for the date (you still have to do that!), keep a bit of distance between the two of you. You can put out your hand and sort of do a hand-shaking thing. Or you can lean in quickly and kiss your date on the cheek. If you don't want to do either of those things, just keep your distance—your date should get the message.

If they don't, and they try to kiss you anyway, just be sure and turn your head so they miss your mouth. You can tolerate a kiss on the cheek. You've probably been kissed by aunts and uncles you weren't all that crazy about, and that quick turn of the head works then, doesn't it?

The good thing about bad dates—they come to an end.

THE NOT-SO-LIKEABLE LIKE-OBJECT

If you don't want to go out with your date again, you've got to be honest about it from the word go. If you're wishy-washy, or you send out mixed signals, this person is going to keep asking you out again and again. It may be the hardest thing in the world for you to do, but you've really got to be frank and honest about your feelings. Thank your date for the evening, but be clear that you don't think you want to go out with them again. You're going to cause hurt feelings—there's no two ways about it—but unless you're clear and blunt, your date will assume you still like him or her, and that you want to continue dating.

Another plan of action is to put off the "I don't want to date you again" news until your date asks you out again. This is actually an excellent plan—after all, why bring up a sore subject until you absolutely have to.

Yet another option is the third-party plan—get a close friend to convey your feelings to your date. This is a very nifty option for people like me, who have issues with confrontation. You'll get your point across without actually having to face your date.

Let's face it—telling your date that you're not interested in seeing him or her anymore is not the easiest thing in the world to do, but if it's how you feel, you've got to be honest about it.

Of course, all this stuff goes two ways—your date may not want to go with you again! Remember what I said before—don't take your date's rejection to heart. Sure it hurts your feelings, but it simply means your date realizes the two of you don't have as much in common as he or she thought. Whatever you do, don't start thinking "I'm too fat," "He doesn't like my hair," or "I shouldn't have said (whatever) during dinner." You're fine just the way you are, and your opinions and thoughts are what make you such a special and unique individual. If your date doesn't want to go out again, it's probably all for the best. Two people both have to like each other a lot for a cool, healthy relationship to develop. It doesn't work if one of you isn't into it.

"WILL I SEE YOU AGAIN?"

Just as one nerve-racking situation passes, another one rears its ugly head. Now you're probably stressing over this little worry—will I be seeing my date again?

Now of course, you'll probably *see* your date again—at school, at your church group, or wherever it was you saw him or her before. But you know what you're really asking is, will you be going out on another date?

When the Date's Over

As I mentioned before, when your date ends—and you want to know when the next one will begin—remember to tell your date what a good time you had. You can say, "I hope we can do this again soon" and let your date run with the ball. If you're feeling really confident, you might say something like, "Do you think you might want to catch another movie next week?"—that's a clear indication of your feelings, and it also gets the plans in motion again.

But even if you've had the times of your lives, don't be surprised if plans for another date aren't made that very minute. Sometimes it's just nice to enjoy things one date at a time— walk into your house remembering the wonderful night you had, not stressing about what the future will bring.

The Second Time Around . . . Don't Think So!

There are some dates you can't wait to see again—and some you'd really prefer never to see again. Sometimes a date reveals a side of himself or herself that you really don't like, and you just know you're not going to want to give them a second chance. Here are some examples of obvious loser types:

The cheater

During the date, your like-object mentions that he or she has a significant other. Nice of him or her to mention it now, don't you think? You might not want to believe it. Or, you might think you're so fab that your crush is going to ditch that "other" and start an awesome relationship with you. But think about it—do you really want to date someone who's already a known cheater? What makes you think he or she won't cheat on you one day? Cut this one loose!

The secretive sort

Your date is over, and you know nothing new about your like-object—he or she wouldn't even tell you what their favorite salad dressing is! If you've got the feeling that your

crush is keeping secrets, big or small, you probably should think twice about going out again. It's normal for someone to not spill all their secrets on a first date, but if your like-object isn't telling you anything at all, there's a problem.

The major offender

Everyone has certain principles and beliefs—these beliefs are a part of what make you you. If your date starts spouting ideas and opinions that make you cringe, it's obvious you're not going to want to hang with him or her. And if your date starts making fun of the things you believe in, it's doubly obvious. Don't make excuses for your date, no matter how much you might have liked him or her.

The cusser

I don't know about you, but nothing makes me more uncomfortable than being with someone who spews obscenities every five minutes. When someone can't put together a sentence without adding some choice curse words, it's a sure sign that that person is a lamebrain. Don't you be embarrassed about feeling uncomfortable—tell your date it bothers you. If they don't stop, make a note—this is a date you want to ditch pronto.

The prize fighter

There's nothing wrong with expressing opinions, even if your opinions are different from the ones your date holds. In fact, debating and discussing opinions are a fun and cool way to get to know one another. But if your date goes postal every time the two of you disagree, put yourself on notice—a bad temper is not an attractive trait, and someone who blows up over minor disagreements is not someone you're going to want to spend a lot of time with. Tell your date to take a chill pill and say no to a second date.

LYNN'S STORY: A PERFECT DATE

"My first date will always be one of the best memories I ever had. I went to play mini-golf with this guy I really liked—it was silly, and so much fun. We didn't stop laughing for a minute! When the date was over, he walked me home and kissed me goodnight at the door. It was so romantic, and I was all shaky when he kissed me. I thought it was the most perfect first date ever!"

The pig

OK, so your date spilled sauce on his or her shirt—no biggie. But if your date came to the door looking sloppy, that's a red flag. First dates are about first impressions, and if your like-object came to your door looking dirty, that means your date doesn't think much of you—or of himself or herself! You can't judge a book by its cover (the person might be really nice and have a heart of gold underneath all that grit—you just have to scrub them down with a Brillo pad to find out!), but it's safe to assume that if someone can't take the time to groom themselves properly, there's something rotten in Denmark.

The bore

This is a tough one. Your like-object might still be a perfectly wonderful person, but during the date you discover that talking to him or her is like taking a Sominex sleeping pill. Put a good spin on it—you just don't have enough in common. But if you found your mind wandering when your date talked or, worse still, you found yourself nodding off, it's clear you two are not meant for each other.

The green-eyed monster

So you're on your first date, and your crush is already showing his or her jealous side. He snapped at you when your best guy buddy said hello to you at the movie theater; she gave you heck because an old girlfriend just happened to be at the pizza parlor. You might be a little flattered by the attention, or you might think, "Hey, this person must really like me a lot." But beware—jealousy is an ugly trait, and if your date is showing signs of it at this stage, he or she is going to be a real treat later on in the relationship.

The violent type

If your date casually mentions that he likes mutilating small animals, remember—this is the sign of a serial killer, not a great boyfriend. If your crush tells you about the fight she got into after the basketball game last week (and how she gave someone a really primo black eye) this is a signal that she's a little wacky. Don't brush these signs away, ignore them, or laugh them off. They're real and they're nasty, and you don't want to associate with this type of person.

FRANK'S STORY: GREAT UP UNTIL THE END

"I remember my first date was with this girl named Lisa. We went bowling with a bunch of friends, and it was cool. Then we all went to the arcade together, and she beat me at the *Jurassic Park* game, which was also fine. Anyway, the whole day was great, until I walked her home and tried to kiss her. I guess she didn't really want me to, because she turned her face and we sort of bumped noses. It kind of hurt! I think she just liked me as a friend, which kind of stunk because I really liked her. But we did stay friends after that—we just never talked about the bumping!"

Mr. or Ms. Wrong

Sometimes you can't put your finger on the reason you and your date didn't click. Something was just missing—there was no spark between the two of you. You didn't share enough interests or your date just wasn't what you expected. In these cases, you might want to give your like-object another chance—maybe the second date will set off fireworks.

Who Is This Person?

In the last chapter, I mentioned that sometimes after a date your like-object might start acting a little weird. You might be acting a little weird also. Weird how? Well, maybe you're kind of avoiding each other. Maybe you're not chatting up a storm outside your locker anymore. Maybe you feel shyer than you normally would around each other. Maybe you're avoiding being in the same stratosphere.

These feelings (and this behavior) may be totally lame, but they're normal. Sometimes, when a guy really likes a girl (and vice versa, of course), he gets extra shy around her. And after a date, he may get shyer still—after all, he's vulnerable isn't he? He's expressed feelings of affection to his like-object, and now he's probably afraid that all his buddies are going to start teasing him about it.

Girls aren't immune to silly behavior either. After a date, a girl might feel self-conscious around the guy. She might also get the teasing treatment from her friends. When I went out on my first date, I made the mistake of telling too many people, and before I knew it, even my homeroom teacher was teasing me!

It's important to remember this weird behavior is normal, and the only way to battle it is to behave like yourself. Treat your date just the way you always did. If it was your habit to drop by his locker before geometry class, do it. If you always walk with her from the cafeteria to gym class, do it. You'll be able to get over the awkwardness more easily if you just act the way you normally would.

THE GUY THING

Despite all the progress humankind has made throughout the years, we are still unable to do anything about what I will call "the guy thing." The guy thing is where a guy will hang out with his buds and totally ignore the girl he likes—and that can mean the girl he's just gone out on a date with. A girl will walk by her guy, and he'll totally turn his back on her so he can hear what his buddies are saying about their favorite sports team. The girl will feel completely embarrassed and humiliated, convinced the guy she likes hates her guts. Then when he meets her at three o'clock to walk home, he's perfectly perfect again.

This bothers girls to no end, and they are pretty clear about how much they hate this behavior. But for some reason, generation after generation of guys keep doing it. I could never understand why this behavior bothers girls so much—even though it did bother me a lot, I have to admit.

The fact is guys do not want to appear vulnerable or less guy-like in front of their friends. They want their friends to think that the girl they like is no big deal. They might bring a girl roses and write her poetry in their spare time, but in front of the guys, they gotta keep it cool.

If you're a girl, and the guy you just dated is doing this, don't stress—it doesn't mean he hates you, and it doesn't mean he doesn't think you're special. In fact, it has nothing to do with you at all—it's like a role he has to play in front of his friends. If he's giving you the guy-thing treatment, just smile and ignore it. It's how he treats you when you're together that's really important, after all.

The only time this behavior is completely unaccept-able is if he and his friends are goofing on you or teasing you when they're all together. If his friends are making fun of you, and he's just standing there letting them, then you've got a problem—like, he's a slimeball and you need to dump him.

But if they're all just hanging out, and he's trying to pre-tend he doesn't notice you, don't worry so much—he notices you all right, and he wishes he were with you at that moment. He just doesn't want his friends to know how much you mean to him.

WHEN YOUR FRIENDS HATE YOUR DATE

Ah, friends—our best friends—where would we be without them? Actually, sometimes we probably wish we *were* without them!

Your best friends are the people you share your secret thoughts with. They're the people who are there for you when things get rough, the people who support you when you need a helping hand. And sometimes, they're the people who hate your date!

When your friends don't like the person you're dating, you're in a majorly rough position. If they think he's a loser, they'll tell ya—over and over again. If they think she's a snob, they'll give you examples until you're sure you went out with her much nicer twin sister.

One thing you gotta know is that your friends care about you, and they don't want to see you get hurt. They might hon-estly have your best interests at heart, and they might be able to see things you can't—like what a loser your date really is! Sometimes your friends will be right and you will be wrong.

But sometimes, your friends might be jealous. They might envy the fact that you've found someone special, and they might be out to spoil it. Or, they might resent the time you're spending with your like-object—time you used to spend with them.

In fact, you might be the one causing this resentment. Think about it—are you talking about your like-object constantly, interrupting your friends to mention how cute your crush looks today? Are you blowing your friends off so you can spend more time with your like-object? If the answer is yes, you might want to rectify the situation, and be sure to make plenty of quality time for your nearest and dearest buds.

There's another situation that might be arising, and that is, your friends might not understand what you see in your crush. If your like-object is shy, your friends may think he or she is lame. If your crush is smart, your friends might think he or she is an egghead. If the one you like is not "the type you usually go for," your friends may be asking, "What's this all about?" The truth is, you may see something special in your crush that others can see—that's what makes your crush yours, not theirs.

If your friends really don't like the person you're dating, sit back and think about your situation for a while. Do they have legitimate concerns? Is your date mean to you? Does he or she treat you badly? Think about whether or not your friends could be right. If they're not, and you really like the person you're dating, be honest with your friends. Tell them they're out of line, and that you think they're being nasty for no reason. Tell them you appreciate their concern, but that you really like this person, and you're really hoping to develop a good relationship with your like-object. Tell your friends that you'll always remain tight, but that now you've got a special person in your life. If they really are your good friends, they'll understand and love you anyway.

HOW TO GET IT BACK TOGETHER WITH YOUR DATE

So you've had your first date, and it went great—and now your date is acting like the two of you never met. You might be thinking, "Who is this person? This is not the person I went out with on Saturday night!"

If you really like the person you went out with, and you want to continue dating him or her, you've got to be yourself and get both of you back to a pre-date feeling again.

I've been big-time guilty of screwing up after a first date. Once I had a date with a guy, and I thought it went really well. The next time I saw him, he acted like he'd never seen me before—I mean, he totally ignored me! So I basically flipped out. I started following him around, going "Is everything OK? Is everything OK?" When he said yes, I flipped out more—'cause everything was obviously not OK, right? I started calling him, leaving messages on his answering machine, and basically acting like stalker supreme. Finally, when I asked him to please tell me what was wrong, he said, "I can't handle this!" and stormed away.

He was a jerk, but so was I. When I realized he was having after-date anxiety, I should have given him space. I should have kept my cool and acted like my normal, charming, and adorable self. I should have kept my dignity, and simply said, "Oh well. I had a good time, and I thought he did too, but if he's acting like this, he must be a total cretin. I'll just wait and see if he calls me again—and I certainly shouldn't follow him around like a puppy dog."

I know. It's hard when you really like someone. You want to be reassured that everything is all right, and that they still like you, and that you're going to have another great date. But the best way to make that happen is to step back from the situation and keep your cool. No one likes to be chased around, and no one likes to feel like they're being swallowed up.

If you just act the way you always did—the way you did when you first attracted your like-object in the first place—you will see all those post-date nerves totally disappear. Once you both realize that you're still the same people you always were, you can relax enough to talk about future dates.

WHEN IT'S REALLY RIGHT

Of course, there are those awesome occasions, those really amazing first dates that lead to serious boyfriend-girlfriend relationships. How do you know if you've had one of those? It is when, after a date, you and your like-object still feel perfectly comfortable together—there are no nerves or anxiety, neither of you is ignoring the other, and neither of you is hiding out with your friends. Everything is just perfect. You make plans for a second date, and you're totally happy to be in one another's company. That's called a keeper. And when you find a keeper, you won't need any more advice from me—you'll just know it's really right.

Dating by the Dozen

14

PLAYING THE FIELD: PROS AND CONS

Once you've been out in the dating scene for awhile, you may have to make this seriously tough decision—should I date one person exclusively, or should I date more than one person at a time? It's a decision that deserves some real thought and consideration.

Dating more than one person at a time used to be called "playing the field" (a phrase that's still used pretty regularly). Years ago, young people were often urged to "play the field" in order to "sow one's oats." (Oh see, once you get caught up in clichés you just can't stop, can you?) Basically, the method behind the madness was this—if you date lots of different people when you're young, you'll be totally ready to settle down and get serious with the person you intend to marry. Whether it worked or not, we'll never really know, will we?

For some reason, it's socially more acceptable for guys to date several girls at one time than it is for girls to date a bunch of guys. The guys are called players; the girls are called . . . usually something else, and something not so nice.

There are several reasons that someone might want to date more than one person at a time. The first is, they're a bit insecure, and dating a bunch of people at the same time makes them feel like a big deal. The second is they really, truly like two people at the same time. For example, maybe date "one" is smart and funny, while date "two" is emotional and shy—combine the two, and you've got the perfect date! Still, a third scenario revolves around someone who's been in a relationship for awhile, and who meets someone new and exciting. Suddenly, there are two like-objects showing up at the door! The fourth story revolves around someone who is majorly shallow and superficial—someone who treats others like trophies or toys. This type of person just likes the thrill of the conquest, and enjoys being known as a "playa" among friends.

The key to successful dual-dating is honesty—if you're going to date more than one person, you've got to tell each and every one of them the truth! I know that sounds awful, doesn't it? But it's vital if you want to avoid unpleasant situations and fights.

Of course, when you're dating two or more people at a time, you're inviting all sorts of risks. If you start favoring one over the other, for example, you're bound to cause some hurt feelings. And even if you are honest about what you're doing, you can find yourself stumbling into confusing situations—not the least of which is forgetting which date you're planning to meet on a given night!

The plus side? Well, dating several people definitely keeps the dating casual, which means it might be the way to go if you want to avoid a serious relationship. It also gives you a chance to get to know more people, which is always cool. If you're really involved in something that means a lot to you—like sports, drama, music, or academic pursuits—it might be a good idea to avoid commitment, and enjoy dating lots of different people who share your interests.

If you find yourself interested in dating more than one person, the first thing you might want to do is examine your motives—why is this something I want to do? Is there something missing within me that I'm trying to fill with all this dating activity? If you are already dating someone, and your interest is sparked by another, you might want to ask yourself, "Do I really want to risk losing the person I'm with now by dating someone else?"

That Not-So-Nice Name

As I mentioned before, guys have an easier time when it comes to dating more than one person at a time. When girls do it, they sometimes find themselves with what is known as a "bad reputation"—to be blunt, girls are often called "sluts" if they're seen dating more than one guy. When guys do it, they're called a "playa" and are generally greeted by high-fives from their friends.

Why the double standard? For years, girls were expected to behave in a certain pristine and innocent way, and that meant saving themselves for one special guy. Boys, on the other hand, were urged to "sow their wild oats," and "have as much fun as they can" before settling down with one girl. Of course, the mystery throughout history has been—who are those guys sowing their wild oats with, if not girls, who are then called sluts? It's a situation that has confused humankind throughout history.

There's really only one plan to end the absurd double-standard, and that's

DOUBLE-TIME DATING—THUMBS UP

Allison's Story

"When I was in high school, I was dating two guys at the same time—David and James. David was a sweet guy. He wrote poetry and he loved going to the movies; James was more athletic. He was on the basketball team, and he really liked taking me out roller-blading or hiking. I liked both of them a lot, and I was always honest with them both—they each knew I was dating someone else. I had a really great time with both guys, and I was glad I got the chance to get to know both of them. I wasn't really serious about either of them, and when I was a senior, and ready to leave for college, I just sort of broke up with both of them!"

DOUBLE-TIME DATING—THUMBS WAY DOWN

Jamal's Story

"I dated two girls at the same time, and neither of them knew about the other. I was always lying to one when I was out with the other one, and vice versa. I was really full of myself—I thought I was all that and everything because I had two girls fighting over me! And then one day I was out with Kim, and I called her Alisa, and she just wailed on me but good! I mean, she started smacking me and yelling, 'Who's Alisa? Who's Alisa? Are you cheating on me?' Of course, I said 'No way!' but she didn't believe me and she dumped me. And then I realized that I really liked Kim a lot, and I didn't like Alisa that much, so I lost a great girl because I wanted to be this big player!"

to chill with the nasty names. If a girl is dating more than one guy at a time, it's really the business of only her and the guys. It would also help if you hold guys to a higher standard—when a guy starts acting like a playa, why not chew him out instead of congratulating him?

My Take on the Dual-Dating Thing

I have to say that personally, I think dating more than one person at a time is a little lame. To me, it implies a lack of respect and consideration for others. After all, those people you're dating have feelings equal to yours, and it's really not cool to play with them just because you think you can get away with it.

More importantly though, it's totally confusing to date more than one person. It takes a lot of planning, a lot of preparations, and maybe even some flow-charting. You've got to remember who likes sad movies, who hates bowling, who's allergic to seafood, and who likes to sing along with the country-music cassettes you keep in the car.

Even more important than that is the emotional confusion you will feel if you start juggling dates like they were hackey sacks. You're never going to be able to build a strong, caring relationship with any of your gazillion dates, because you're never going to spend enough time with any one of them. You won't be able to see the relationship develop and progress the way you would if you were concentrating on one date at a time. And finally, you won't notice when things go wrong—like, if you're dating three people at the same time, and person number one is starting to get on your nerves, you won't realize it until it's too late—and you may have lost number one's friendship forever.

But, if you're determined to play that field, remember to be honest with all the parties involved. That will save a lot of potential heartache for everyone.

Should I or Shouldn't I?

15

OK, so you probably know what this chapter is all about . . . or do you? The fact is, a lot of teens think they know all about sex, when in actuality, they know very little.

Oh sure, you may know all about the mechanics of sex—what goes where and things like that. But do you really know what sex is all about on an emotional level? Do you know what it means to you? Do you know if you're ready for it?

IF IT FEELS GOOD . . .

Let's face facts—getting physical with someone you like a lot is fun—it feels nice. Kissing, hugging, touching, and caressing are all wonderful things. And once you've started getting close to someone, it sometimes feels like you never want to stop.

But sex is more than just doing something that feels good—it is (or should be) a major step, something you share with someone you love. It should be special; it should be loving, warm, and intimate. It's not something you want to do with just anyone.

For many young people, the question of "should I or shouldn't I?" weighs heavily. That's normal. As your body grows and matures, feelings start to emerge that tell you sex is something you want to pursue. And hey, that's normal too. Remember, many, many years ago, people your age were already starting to marry and have kids, so it's natural that your body is preparing for that.

But in today's world, things are very different. People are waiting to marry. Most people wait until they've completed all their education and are working in their chosen profession before they even think about getting married. And even if people do marry young, they're still waiting longer than our ancestors did.

That's why the issue of sex is so difficult and so pressing. People are waiting to make loving, permanent commitments, but their bodies are still urging them toward closeness.

Another relatively modern phenom is that young people start dating earlier and spend more time in the dating phase of their lives than our grandparents did. We spend more time doing casual dating—in fact, our grandparents might not have done any casual dating at all. This means that you might date a lot of different people in the course of your teen years—a lot of people you probably won't want to have sex with.

All these issues make for some complicated questions: Are you ready to have sex? If not now, when? Do you want to remain a virgin until you're married, or until you find a committed, loving partner? Do you really need to think about this at all right now?

ARE YOU READY FOR THIS?

One of the biggest mistakes young people make regarding sex is that they simply don't think before they act. (Actually, this is the biggest mistake *EVERYONE* makes regarding sex!)

Of course, it's hard to think rationally when you're making out with your boyfriend or girlfriend, and you're feeling all these overpowering urges. It's easier to just do it than to think it through. But think it through you must, if you want to make the right decisions.

One of the first things you must realize is that just because you're dating someone, it doesn't automatically mean you should be having sex with that person. Say it again—dating does not equal sex! They are not the same thing, and they shouldn't be thought of in the same way. Dating is fun, it can be casual, and it should be easy and simple. Sex is fun, yes—but it's definitely not casual, and it can be anything but easy and simple.

A lot of young women say they've dated someone who's tried to pressure them into having sex. They've heard a lot of creative (and totally garbage-filled) lines from the guys they've gone out with—lines designed to "guilt" them into taking a step they weren't ready to take.

It bears repeating that guilt is not a real romantic feeling. It's also not a good reason to agree to give in to sex. If you're feeling guilty, or pressured, about getting physical, that's actually reason enough to put the brakes on and say no. That means if your date says. . .

"I spent a lot of money on this date. I expect to get something in return."

"I'm your boyfriend aren't I? Don't you think it's time you treated me like one?"

"If you don't do it with me, I'll break up with you."

"Hey, everybody's doing it!"

. . . you should get away from your date pronto.

You see, if someone really loves you and cares about you and your feelings, they won't pressure you, and they certainly won't equate spending some money on a movie and dinner with sex. And quite frankly, if you think any of those lines is a turn-on, you're not playing with a full set of crayons. Romance, love, and intimacy are not about trade-offs, or pay-offs.

HOW DO YOU KNOW IF YOU'RE READY?

One of the toughest questions you'll ever have to deal with is, "Am I ready for sex?" And guess what? If you're asking it, the answer is probably "No."

Sex is not without risks, and you probably know some of those risks already. Pregnancy is a major one, of course. Even if you take precautions and use some form of birth control, you are not 100 percent protected from the risk of pregnancy—that's a fact. Are you ready for that risk? I doubt it.

Another risk is Sexually Transmitted Disease, or STD. The one we hear the most about is AIDS, which is Acquired Immune Deficiency Syndrome, and is a life and death disease. Other STDs are genital herpes and gonorrhea—and there are a host of others. These diseases are serious and, if you get them, require a doctor's care for treatment. You can't run into the drugstore and buy a bottle of pills to cure them. All STDs affect your life—your health, your future sexual life, and your ability to bear children. They're not colds that go away. They're diseases that will change your life forever and, in the case of AIDS, sometimes fatally. Using condoms (also known as rubbers and a bunch of other unattractive names) can help protect you, but again, the key word is "can"—nothing is 100 percent effective.

Not very romantic, is it?

When people talk about the risks of sexual activity, they're usually concentrating on pregnancy or disease. But what's usually overlooked is the risk to your emotional health, well being, and self-esteem. There's no contraceptive to protect you from these risks.

Far too often, young people jump into sex on a whim, not realizing that there might be an emotional price to pay. Too many teens engage in sex, believing they're doing it with a loving, caring partner, only to find they've been used. (Again, this is not just a teen thing—adults have to deal with this issue too.) It's emotionally devastating to give yourself to a partner, only to find out that partner is not the least bit concerned

"EVERYBODY'S DOING IT"

What do you say to this argument?

You could say, "I'm not everybody. I'm me."

You could say, "Are you having sex with everybody?"

You could say, "Not that I've heard."

What you should not—never, ever—say is "You're right! Let's do it!"

When I was in high school, I heard that this mythical "everybody" was doing everything, from having sex to taking drugs to running naked on the football field. Funny thing was, I never saw anyone in my own group of friends doing any of those things. In fact, I learned that if someone tells you "everyone is doing it," the chances are, no one is.

Even if it were true—say everyone else was doing "it" (whatever "it" is)—does that automatically mean you have to, or even want to? I hate to use this annoying cliché, but if everyone jumped off the roof of your school, would you really want to? Why exactly is "everyone's doing it" such a powerful persuader? Because it zones in on your need to fit in, your need to be accepted. No one wants to feel left out, and no one wants to feel like a loser. That's why so many young people give in to this stupid, flawed argument.

The best way to deal with "everyone else is doing it" is to remember one thing—you're not everyone else, you're you. You are the one who has to make decisions about your life. You're the one who has to make the choices. If you give in and agree to have sex, and then regret your decision, is "everyone" going to have to deal with it? No, you are.

about your feelings. Many young women told me about their own experiences:

Lori's Story

"I thought I was in love with this guy—we'd been dating about three months, and I was really serious about him, so I decided it was OK to have sex with him. He'd really been pressuring me, saying it was OK, he loved me. After we did it, he got really cold with me. He didn't talk to me the whole way home. The next day at school, I heard he'd told all his friends we'd had sex, but he still wasn't talking to me—in fact, he never talked to me again."

Ann Marie's Story

"My best friend was having sex with her boyfriend, so I figured it was OK to do it with my boyfriend. It really wasn't very nice—in fact, it hurt a lot. When it was over, I was so sorry I'd done it. I realized that I did it only because my friend was doing it, like it was some kind of competition."

Heidi's Story

"After I had sex with my guy, things were never the same. We stopped going out on dates—all he wanted to do was have sex. And he stopped treating me in that special way he used to treat me. I think that once he'd gotten sex from me, he didn't think I needed to be treated with respect anymore. He started making fun of me, saying that I was fat and ugly, and that no one else would ever want to go out with me. He told me that if I broke up with him, I'd never meet anyone else. It was really bad—I mean, I actually believed him! When I finally did break up with him, it took me a long time to feel like myself again."

Ellen's Story

"I really loved my boyfriend a lot, so when we started having sex, I just thought it was this natural progression of our relationship. The problems started when I thought I was pregnant—my period was a few days late. I was totally sweating it out for those three days, let me tell you. When I told my boyfriend, I thought he was going to kill me. I'd never seen him get angry before, but this time he was enraged. He started screaming at me, and telling me how horrible I was, and how this was all my fault—even though he was there too! When my period came, and I realized I wasn't pregnant, he was so relieved, and he became totally normal again. But I'd learned my lessons big time—I broke up with him and told him I never wanted to see him again. He couldn't understand why. He said everything was fine, so why was I screwing up our relationship. He didn't understand that he was the one who'd screwed everything up."

As you can see, there are some serious emotional issues to consider when you're making the decision to have sex. If you're not certain whether you can handle these issues, it's best to wait.

A NO-BRAINER

Of course, one decision you can make right this very minute is this: you will not have sex on a first date, ever! That's a total no-brainer, by the way, whether you're 13, 18, 35, or 55! Sex on the first date is never a good option.

Sex is supposed to be something you share with someone you love. Do you fall in love with someone on the first date? Not usually. I might be a little over-the-top here, but I don't necessarily even want to share a bag of popcorn with someone on a first date.

A first date is all about getting to know someone—so is a second and a third date, by the way. When you're going out with someone for the first time, you're really spending time with a stranger. You don't know anything about this person, other than you think they're nice-looking and you like their smile or some other totally superficial thing like that. The purpose of dating is to see whether you share values, interests, and ideals—that discovery process is part of the dating fun.

People who have sex on the first date confuse me. I mean, think about it, you wouldn't wash another person's clothes on the first date, you wouldn't rummage through their closets or their refrigerator and you probably wouldn't even use their hairbrush, but you'd consider having sex with them? Come on, be sensible here!

Remember that sex is about sharing your most valuable possessions—your body, you mind, and your spirit. Don't treat it casually, like going to the movies. It should be special.

NOW FOR SOMETHING COMPLETELY DIFFERENT

This may seem like another no-brainer, but I very rarely see it discussed. The first time you have sex isn't always the greatest experience in the world. In fact, it's often painful, uncomfortable, and embarrassing.

For a young woman, the first sexual experience is almost always painful. Not like losing a limb painful, mind you, but painful nonetheless. Your body is doing something it hasn't done before, and it takes time and loving care to prepare it properly.

For a young man, it's almost always a little embarrassing— things don't always go the way you think they're going to, no matter how carefully you've planned it.

Sounds positively sexy, huh? For these reasons, sex is always better when the two people doing it are in love. The person you love will help you through the uncomfortable patches, and because they love you, there will be less embarrassment. That's why so many young people do choose to wait.

WHEN YOU CHOOSE ABSTINENCE

Choosing to remain a virgin is a totally personal decision. It's not something you have to shout out to the world; it's not a pledge you need to make publicly. It's all about you, and about the value you place on your body and your heart.

If you choose to remain a virgin, either until you marry or until you meet someone you want to share your life with, you should be proud of your decision, but you needn't tell everyone around you about it. It doesn't have to be a mission—it's simply your choice.

If you become involved with someone, and the sex question rears its head, you should be honest with that person—tell them about the decision you've made and why it's important to you. Tell them that pressuring you or trying to "guilt" you into sex will not change your mind, it will only force you to end the relationship. Be clear, be firm, and be true to yourself. Don't give out mixed messages—don't start getting into behavior that might make the other person think you're changing your mind. Stress how important your choice is to you.

If your friends start teasing you or pressuring you, simply tell them that this is a choice you've made. Don't get into arguments or debates about it—remember this is something you're doing for yourself. Don't allow others to make you feel "bad" about your decision, and don't allow their opinions to change your conviction.

Most importantly, remember that you're the one who has to live with your choices. Feel good about the decisions you make for yourself, and remember that those decisions say a lot about the person you want to be.

The Future Should Be Bright

Another thing you should remember is that sex is more than just something you do once—it's something that can affect your future. Pregnancy will change your entire life, and often not for the better. It's the same with STDs—whatever happens afterward, it will probably not be the future you had planned for yourself.

If your life means anything to you, if you have goals and dreams for the future, it's important to concentrate on those goals and dreams. Having a baby probably means you will not be able to finish your education, and that means your career plans will have to be tossed away. (Some people do continue their education after having a child, but the majority do not.) So if you have a special life planned for yourself, it's simply easier to do everything you can to avoid unwanted pregnancies—and that means waiting for sex.

When No Means No

Once you've made the decision to wait for sex, you face another problem—how do you stick to your decision, and how to make sure others respect it.

As I mentioned before, it's important to take yourself seriously when you make a decision regarding sex. In other words, once you've decided to refrain from sex, and you're happy and comfortable with that choice, do not allow room for discussion or debate. The important thing to remember is that this choice has everything to do with you—and that means you have to stand up for yourself.

If your boyfriend or girlfriend is trying to pressure you into having sex, remember the reasons you made your choice in the first place. Remember how important the decision is for you and your future. Say no with conviction—but also with love and care. Remind your significant other that he or she already knows what your answer is going to be—you're saying no to sex for now. And stress that if this pressure continues, you're going to have to rethink the relationship.

Whatever you do, don't allow someone else to dictate what your decision will be. That choice belongs to you—don't give it away.

Dating with Confidence

YOU'VE SAID YES . . .
NOW YOU'RE SORRY

Sometimes, even with the best-made plans, you may give in to the pressure and decide to have sex. Or, you might say yes because you genuinely love your partner and believe sex is the right thing to do. So now it's over, and it was the wrong thing to do.

As you read in the stories from other young women, sex doesn't always end with a romantic song, a kiss goodnight, and the promise of a lifetime of happiness. Sometimes it ends badly, and you're left feeling alone, frightened, and maybe even ashamed. Perhaps your partner turned away from you, or perhaps you just feel, inside, like you've done something wrong.

If you've had sex, and then decide it's not something you want to do again, guess what—you don't have to do it again. If you've experienced sex, and then realized you weren't emotionally ready for the commitment it brings, you can take a step back, re-evaluate your situation, and then let your partner know you'd rather wait before doing it again. If your boyfriend or girlfriend cares for you, it won't be a problem—if he or she doesn't, and refuses to understand your feelings, it's time to dump 'em.

Remember that sometimes having sex changes the relationship between you and your partner. You might be nervous with one another—it might even feel like you don't know the other person at all (something adults also experience—it's not a teenage phenomenon). Your boyfriend might behave like a total idiot—he might tell all his friends about what you did, or he might start acting like a stranger. Your girlfriend might look for ways to avoid you, to avoid talking about what happened.

This is where that love and commitment thing comes in again. If you and your partner are really meant to be together, you'll be able to work through these uncomfortable feelings through conversation and loving reassurances. You'll be able to understand that something has changed—you've progressed to a new, deeper relationship—and you'll know that the other person will still always be there for you. And if it's true love, you'll feel closer and more together than before.

THE FINAL WORD ON SEX

Yeah right. Like there's a "final word."

Whether or not to have sex is a deeply personal choice. It comes from a place deep inside you. You make this choice based on moral and religious values, family values, and personal values. This choice should have nothing to do with what your friends think, or even what your boyfriend or girlfriend thinks—it's something you must choose for yourself. And once you make that choice, it's up to you to stay true to it. If you choose to wait, remember, it's not a "forever" thing—it's just for now, just for today. If you choose to have sex, remember it's a major step, one that involves precaution and care.

And finally, don't waste sex on someone who doesn't deserve you. Never do it to "hold on" to someone, or to "prove" your love for them. Sex isn't like sharing your lunch—it's sharing you. It's something that's way too important to toss away on some loser who's trying to pressure you or "guilt" you into it. Sex really is best when it's shared between two people in love—that's not a moral judgment or statement, it's a real fact. If you wait to find just the right person, you'll definitely be happier in the long run.

The Dark Side of Dating

Up until now, we've been having a pretty good time talking about dating—the fun things you can do and plan, the best ways to prepare for a successful date, and the things you should do to avoid having a lame one. Unfortunately, these days there are lots of other things to think and worry about when you get into the dating scene—and now it's time to talk about some of those things.

No doubt, your parents or members of your family have already warned you about things that can happen to you when you go out with someone you don't know that well. You may have dismissed their worries and fears; perhaps you even said to yourself, "Nothing like that can ever happen to me!"

But the fact is, tens of thousands of young people find themselves in dangerous, often terrifying situations because they dismissed these fears and believed they were indestructible. Unless you are aware of the dangerous things that can happen to you, you won't be able to protect yourself against them.

You may dismiss these warnings as "paranoid," but the truth is that taking just a few safety precautions can save you a lifetime of misery. And if you're worried about being "uncool," listen up—there's nothing more uncool than being seriously hurt (physically and emotionally) or dead. Avoiding a bad situation and protecting yourself from harm is the coolest thing you can ever do. And don't ever forget that.

STALKING

Stalking is often the subject of melodramatic made-for-TV movies and majorly bad big-screen films. You know the kind I mean—the crazed, curly-haired female goes bonkers over some guy and starts following him around. At first, she just professes her great love for him. Then, when he rejects her, she boils his bunny in the crock pot. Well, this *Fatal Attraction* scenario may be a total crock (in more ways than one), but stalking is a real problem for a lot of people, young and old.

A person becomes a stalker when he or she is rejected by someone. Instead of dealing with the rejection, they become obsessed with the object of their affection. They begin to follow their crush, leave notes, call, and then hang up—anything to get their crush's attention.

The truth about stalking? Men become stalkers more often than women do. That might be because guys have a tougher time taking rejection, or because they feel a need to be in control of situations and people. But girls shouldn't get too cocky about that, because they can definitely become stalkers too. Stalking isn't a guy versus girl thing—it's a very dangerous emotional situation that anyone can find themselves falling into.

Stalking has very little to do with love and affection, and everything to do with power. The stalker wants complete control of the crush's life. In fact, the stalker kind of gets off on the fear he or she inflicts on the like-object.

Stalkers might not always seem dangerous—sometimes they're simply annoying, like the girl who keeps showing up at your soccer games, or the guy who keeps leaving notes in your locker. Scary or not, you should always report this kind of behavior to your parents and, if it happens in school, to a school official you trust. Someone that starts off as annoying can turn into someone frightening in a blink of an eye.

What If You're the Stalker?

So . . . that explanation about stalking . . . that has absolutely no connection to your life, right? I mean, you're not a stalker, are you?

Hopefully, you're not the kind of person who goes crazy and boils the bunny. But have you ever exhibited any stalker-type behavior of your own?

I know I have! When I was in high school, and going through my long and (by now) extremely boring crush on Jerry, I was super-annoying. I got to school early to watch him walk to his locker. I tried to get him to be my lab partner in chemistry class, and when I got my car senior year, I was constantly offering him rides home. But I wasn't a stalker. Or was I?

The fact is, annoying, needy behavior (like the stuff I was doing) is always unattractive. Instead of being just Jackie, I became Jackie the pain in the neck—which is not what you want your crush to call you!

Here's a little test to see if you're exhibiting stalker behavior. Answer the following questions with True or False:

1. You leave your crush notes in his or her locker, on his or her car window, or in his or her mailbox.

It's very important to be aware of the bad things that can happen to you when you're out on a date. Always remember to be careful and cautious, and to take care of yourself. If something bad happens to you, report it to an adult you trust and let that adult take the next step.

But also remember that there are more good people than bad in the world. Try not to ever let fear keep you from meeting new people and having new experiences. If you are cautious, you will be able to have a great time and enjoy your life by living it to the fullest.

2. You "show up" at events when you know your crush will be there—even if you have no interest in the event itself.

3. You call your crush, then hang up when you hear his or her voice on the answering machine.

4. You make elaborate arrangements to make sure you are sitting next to your crush in class.

5. You join a club to be nearer to your crush—even when you have no interest in the activities the club promotes.

6. You walk or ride your bike past your crush's house—a lot.

7. You change your "walking home" route from school so you can pass your crush as he or she is walking home.

8. You ignore your friends whenever your crush walks into the room.

9. Whenever you see your crush-object, you just stare at him or her.

10. You need to know what your crush is doing at every minute of the day—and you use whatever means necessary to find out.

If you answered True to two or more of these questions, you're exhibiting "stalker-type" tendencies.

All right. So you're probably thinking—but I have a crush on this person! Of course I'm acting weird! None of these things sounds particularly weird to me!

Perhaps not, but the truth is, obsessing over your crush (or over someone who rejected you after a date) is not going to get that person interested in you. It's going to make that person think you're nuts.

It's totally normal to get excited over your crush, and at one time or another, everyone exhibits some of the minor stalking behavior I've described. So if you're showing some signs, don't stress—no one's going to think you're off your rocker; most people will understand how you're feeling. The important thing is to recognize what's happening, and to reel yourself in if you find yourself getting really freaky. If your crush is totally obsessing you and taking over every aspect of your life, or if it's affecting the way you deal with your friends, your family, and the rest of your social life, you know it's time to take a step back, take a deep breath, and really think about what's going on. Talk to your friends and see what they think about how you're feeling and how you're acting. They may know just exactly what to say to help you chill out.

So if you have a crush that doesn't know you're alive, or if you've gone on a date with someone who doesn't like you as much as you like them, do yourself a favor. Follow the tips I gave you in Chapter 13 and move on. Don't become a stalker.

DRINKING AND DRUGGING

Despite all the warnings, all the education and all the information given to young people about the dangers of drinking and taking drugs, the fact remains that many teens still do one or both. And believe it or not, the reasons teens give for doing them are the same today as they were thirty years ago:

- ✔ *Peer pressure*—All my friends are doing it, so why shouldn't I?
- ✔ *The "cool" factor*—Drinking and taking drugs make me look cool!
- ✔ *The fun argument*—Hey, I want to have a good time, don't I?

Let's look at these reasons in a reasonable way—and let's start with the fun argument, since that's the easiest one to dispel.

If you need alcohol or drugs to have fun, you're a loser, plain and simple.

Some people think that alcohol and drugs make them the life of the party. They believe that if they take a drink, or smoke a joint, they'll become more social and talkative.

Have you ever tried to talk to someone who's drunk or stoned? They're talkative all right. And they're usually talking about A, their amazing new plan for taking over the world; B, how much they love getting high, or C, how they feel like they're going to throw up in a second (that happens right before they throw up on you or into the fish tank).

Just because drugs and alcohol loosen your tongue, doesn't mean it's making you a whole lot of fun to be with. In fact, in all likelihood, drugs and alcohol are turning you into an annoying babbling idiot. Act like that too often, and no one is going to invite you out much anymore.

Oh, wait a sec—you meant that *you* have more fun when you drink or take drugs. I'm sorry, I wasn't paying attention.

The truth is, if you're drinking or using drugs, there's a very good chance you won't even remember if you had a good time or not! And there's also a very good chance that when you wake up the following morning, you will not be having fun at all. In fact, you'll probably be sick as a dog and have a very angry family to deal with.

The bottom line is, you'll have more fun if you're clear-headed, clear-thinking, and fully able to enjoy yourself—none of which you'll be if you're high.

If you think drinking or drugging makes you look cool, you're an even bigger loser!

Swigging a bottle of beer or smoking a joint doesn't make you look any cooler than sipping a soda or eating a potato chip. It's simply something to do with your hands and your mouth.

And then there's that throwing up thing—which believe me, does not look cool at all. And it smells even worse.

Peer pressure. That's a tough one.

It's always hard to say no when your friends are saying yes. When your friends, and maybe even your date, are drinking and smoking and urging you to join in, it can take tremendous strength of character to say a simple, "No thanks." After all, you might be thinking, if they're doing it, how dangerous can it be?

There's no simple answer to resisting peer pressure. I can sit here and tell you to be strong and to stay true to your beliefs and principles, but I know it's a lot harder when you're surrounded by people and you want to be included in what they're doing.

All I can tell you is this—you're the one who has to live with the consequences of your actions, not your friends. You're the one who might get sick, who might get hurt, and who might get into trouble. And if something happens to you, are you so sure those "friends" who tried to pressure you will be there for you? Possibly—but maybe not!

How to Say No and Keep Your Cool

If you've made the decision to stay away from drugs and alcohol, there are lots of things you can do to stay true to yourself, and lots of ways you can avoid getting dragged into a bad situation because of peer pressure:

Always pour your own drink—If you want to stick with soda, pour it yourself! Don't let anyone else fix a drink for you. You never know what might get splashed in.

Just say no thanks—If someone tries to pressure you into taking a drink or a drug, just smile and say, "No thanks, I'm fine." You can also add, "I may have something later, but this is fine for now." After a while, you'll be surprised—no one will even notice that you're not drinking or using drugs!

If you feel uncomfortable, LEAVE—No one can force you to stay at a party. If you went with friends or a date, and you want to leave, let them know. If they want to stay, get up and call your parents and have them pick you up. If you don't want to call your family, call a taxi and pay for it with your emergency money.

AMY'S STORY: THAT DRINK WAS SO NOT COOL

"I was on a date with this guy I went to school with— he was really cute and nice, and I really liked him a lot. He took me to a party— most of the people there were friends of his, but I knew some people there too, so it was cool. I was having an OK time, until I noticed he was drinking beer. He came over to me and started offering me beer, which I definitely didn't want. He was acting so silly and talking so loud, I was embarrassed for him! I think he was just trying to act cool, you know, to impress me. But the thing that made it exceptionally not cool was that he had driven me to the party, and I knew there was no way I was going to let him drive me home after he'd been drinking. I asked one of the girls I knew to take me home, and she said it was no problem. I was lucky there was someone I could turn to—that guy was a complete jerk."

If you're the one who drove your date to the party, you may have some added aggravation. If your date is having a good time, and doesn't want to leave, you may get "guilted" into staying. Also, this might seem to contradict a rule I told you about earlier— the one about leaving the party with the person you came with.

Under certain conditions, this rule gets blown out of the water. If you're uncomfortable because there's drinking or drug use at a party, and you want to leave because of it, your date should be thoughtful and understanding enough to leave with you. If your date is participating in the activity that's making you uncomfortable, then your date is not someone worth concerning yourself with—someone who really likes you would never force you to stay in a situation that's making you feel antsy.

Drunk (or Drugged) Driving

Every year, tens of thousands of young people are hurt or killed in drunk driving accidents. Despite that staggering number, lots of teens still have no problem getting into a car when the person behind the wheel is drunk or stoned. Why do so many people do such a stupid thing? Very simply—they don't think anything bad can happen to them.

You've already heard the warnings. You already know that getting into the car with a drunk driver is idiotic. But chances are, if the situation came up, you might just do it too. You might not want to make a scene, you might not want to stand up for yourself, or you might feel you have no choice. Whatever the reason, you might get into that car and put your life at risk.

Don't be stupid. You always have choices. Let me add my voice to the ones you've already heard—do not get into a car when the driver is impaired by booze or drugs. Just don't.

Parent pick-up contracts

Making a contract with your parents might sound lame, but lots of teenagers make pick-up contracts with their families, and it can be a great way to show your 'rents how responsible and trustworthy you are.

Basically, the contract works like this—you write up a contract that says something like:

"There may be a time where I will go to a party and there will be drinking going on. Maybe the person I went with will have too much to drink; maybe the party will get out of hand. If I want to leave the party, I will call you—no matter what time it is. You will come and pick me up, no questions asked."

RON'S STORY: NOTHING PRETTY ABOUT IT

"I picked up this girl for a date—we were going to a party. As I was walking her to my car, I noticed she had this big bag with her. She'd snuck out a bottle of vodka from her parents' liquor cabinet to bring to the party. She started drinking on the way there, and she got really drunk at the party. It was weird—she was a really pretty girl, but once she started getting drunk, she didn't look so pretty anymore. After about an hour, she got really sick—which was really disgusting. I drove her home and everything, but you better believe I never went out with her again."

With a contract like this, you will know that your parents are there for you, and are totally available to pick you up and bring you home. You won't ever have to rely on friends or a date (who might have had too much to drink) to drive you home. And your parents will know that you will never put yourself in a dangerous drinking situation.

"Roofies"

When I was a teenager, and I started going to parties, my mom used to tell me, "Always pour your own drink, and never leave your drink unattended. You never know what someone might slip into it." I thought she was totally nuts. I mean, come on, what could someone "slip" into a drink? It sounded completely crazy.

The "something" is called Rohypnol, better known as "Roofies" or "the date rape drug." It's a tiny pill that resembles an aspirin, and it dissolves completely when it's mixed into liquid. And when it dissolves, it is totally odorless and tasteless.

What happens when you drink something that's been spiked with a Roofie? Within ten to thirty minutes (depending on your body weight and how much you've eaten) you will begin to feel dizzy, lightheaded, and sleepy. You may even black-out. Once you're out, you're really out—it's not like a nap. The effect can last for several hours.

Roofies are often called date rape drugs because once you've blacked-out, you're completely vulnerable—many young women who get a drink spiked with a Roofie wake up later and find they've been raped, usually by the person who spiked the drink in the first place.

The best way to protect yourself is to follow my mom's advice. Pour your own drinks. And if you have a drink, and you put it down so you can dance or get something to eat, don't automatically pick it up again. Make yourself a new one. It's also helpful if you stay aware of your surroundings and the people around you—if someone's getting uncomfortably close, take a step away and regain your space. But the most important thing here is to keep an eye on everything you drink. No matter how much you trust the people at the party, the only person you can really trust is yourself, especially when it comes to keeping you safe.

UNWELCOME ADVANCES

It sounds like such an old-fashioned phrase, doesn't it? "Unwelcome advances"—how million years ago! It may sound old-fashioned, but things like this never seem to go out of style, no matter how much we want them to!

An unwelcome advance is pretty easy to spot—it's when your date (or anyone else, for that matter) touches you in a way that makes you feel uncomfortable. It can also be when your date (or anyone else) says something that makes you feel uncomfortable—something that seems too personal, for example. Or perhaps your date might make a suggestion that makes you nervous—that too is an unwelcome advance.

If you are alone with someone who says something that makes you uncomfortable, the best thing to do is get away from that person. Let that person know that you're not enjoying what's being said. Don't make a joke, and try not to giggle—just look the person straight in the eye and tell them that what they said was not appropriate.

Normally, what will happen is your date will get embarrassed and apologize. Perhaps he said what he did because he thought it was a cool thing to say, or perhaps he isn't sure about how to act with you. If he doesn't apologize, tell him you want to be taken home and end the date. And of course, avoid him in the future. If he persists, or repeats the remark, get away from him. If you're alone in a room with him, leave. If you're alone in the car with him, get out of it.

The same rules apply if someone touches you inappropriately. If someone invades your "space" and touches you in a way you don't want to be touched, that's called intrusion. Again, it's important to get away from this person as soon as possible. Don't ever worry about being called a "prude" or about appearing "uncool"—it's important to take care of yourself, and to get away from the person who's causing you alarm. That's what your emergency money is for—get away, call a taxi, or your parents, and get home.

Some of the ways to protect yourself from unwanted advances are:

- ✔ Make sure your first date takes place in a public place, like a restaurant or movie theater, or that you have lots of your friends around.
- ✔ Carry that emergency money!
- ✔ Never leave a party, concert, game, or other social occasion with someone you just met or don't know well.
- ✔ Check out how your date treats you. Does he try to control how you dress or your choice of friends? Does he put you down or insult you? This type of behavior gives you a clue to his personality—he's into power and control. That's the type of guy most likely to try to exert power over you with inappropriate touching or remarks.
- ✔ Trust your instincts. If something about your date makes you feel uncomfortable, nervous, or scared, get out and get away.

Now that I've made you totally paranoid, let me pull back for a sec and tell you again that sometimes guys might make advances that they think are perfectly innocent. They might not realize that what they've done bothers you, or they might have done the same thing to another girl without it causing a problem. Everyone is different, and you might be more uncomfortable about the touchy-feely stuff than someone else is. That's why you've got to be specific. If your date touches you in a way that makes you uncomfortable, let him know immediately so there's no misunderstanding.

And remember, some advances *really* are totally innocent. If your date puts his arm around your shoulder, it's because he likes you and wants to be closer to you. The same goes for holding your hand, or resting a hand on your back. This kind of romantic touching is really nice, and if you're freaking over it, it might be because you really don't like your date as much as you thought you did.

But if your date is grabbing or groping you in ways that really are inappropriate, you've got to open your mouth and let him know. Always know that you have the right to stand up for yourself and protect yourself.

BOYFRIEND OR GIRLFRIEND ABUSE

Did you know that cases of physical abuse between boyfriends and girlfriends are on the rise in this country? More and more teenagers are reporting it, and it's a growing trend among high school students.

Both guys and girls can be the victims of dating violence, although boys are still the overwhelming aggressors in these types of situations.

Dating violence is also about power—the aggressor wants to overpower the victim, and to make the victim dependent and vulnerable. Usually, the victim finds himself or herself unable to get out of the abusive situation because they truly believe they deserve the abuse. The aggressor uses his or her power to weaken the victim, to ensure the victim will not have the confidence to stand up for him or herself.

Violent behavior does not usually happen on the first date—or the tenth. An aggressor will gradually move up to violence. Early warning signs of an abusive boyfriend or girlfriend include:

Verbal abuse—Does your boyfriend call you stupid, lazy, or fat? Does your girlfriend put you down in front of others? These verbal assaults are clear red flags, warning signals that tell you your like-object is trying to "keep you in your place" or wear down your self-confidence.

Control issues—Does your like-object fly into a rage if you're five minutes late? Has your boyfriend ever told you he hates your friends and wishes you'd stop hanging around them? Has your girlfriend ever demanded that you come over "this minute," even if you're doing your homework or some important family chore? These are signs of control issues—your like-object is trying to control you and your behavior, trying to separate you from your friends and family, and trying to keep you in a vulnerable, isolated state. Another red flag.

Undermining—If your boyfriend or girlfriend really likes you, he or she will want to build you up, not drag you down. Does your boyfriend rag on you about your future college plans? Does your girlfriend keep telling you she hopes you don't get accepted to the out-of-town university you've got your heart set on? If your like-object really cared about you, he or she would want what's best for you—not for him or her.

Any of these red flags could be a sign of possible violent behavior in the future. Any time your like-object tries to make you feel less capable, less intelligent, or less worthy, take note—he or she could be exhibiting signals of violent tendencies yet to come. You should rethink your relationship ASAP. No matter how much you like someone, you must be aware of how their behavior is affecting you. Never accept verbal put-downs or insults from someone who is supposed to like you—they are never acceptable.

DATE RAPE

Date rape is not a nice thing to think about and it can be a tough thing to talk about, but it's necessary for you to know what it means and how to avoid it.

Date rape is a topic that can be confusing for many people, but especially for teens. After all, no teenager wants to think of himself or herself as a rapist. But the truth is, on college campuses, more than 90 percent of rape victims knew their assailants. In fact, women are much more likely to be raped by a friend or a date than by a stranger.

Why? Because some guys still believe that if they take a girl out on a date she "owes" him something—that something usually means sex. Some guys think that when a girl says "no" she really means "yes"—that she's playing hard to get. And there are some boys who believe that being aggressive toward a girl makes them more masculine.

Even though lots of attitudes in society have changed, guys often still get the message that they're supposed to be competitive and aggressive. Girls often get the message that they're supposed to be passive and quiet, that they should avoid confrontation. That's why date rape still continues to happen.

Following are some things you can do to protect yourself against date rape:

- ✔ Don't wander off alone with someone you just met or don't know well.
- ✔ Avoid drugs and alcohol. Keep your mind clear and always be aware of what's going on around you.
- ✔ If you feel you are in danger, get to a phone and call your parents—let them pick you up and bring you home.

These suggestions, along with the ones listed under Unwelcome Advances, can help protect you.

SEXUAL HARASSMENT

It's quite possible that when your parents went to school, they never learned about "sexual harassment"—they probably never even heard the phrase. These days, most schools do teach their students about sexual harassment—how to spot it, how to avoid it, and how to report it.

To use legal language, sexual harassment is determined by the following guidelines: behavior that creates an intimidating, hostile, or offensive environment. Sexual harassment used to be just an issue at the workplace, but more and more schools are recognizing that the same kind of behavior can be present in school.

So what does this have to do with you, and your new status as a dating person?

There's an excellent ABC-TV movie called *Boys Will Be Boys* that can answer that question for you more clearly. It tells the story of a girl named Ali, who finds herself the subject of vicious rumors. Things get really bad when a boy she knows writes obscene graffiti about her in the boys' bathroom. The movie tells the story of Ali's struggle to make the school take responsibility and to punish the boy who wrote the graffiti.

The point is, if you go out on a date, and the boy (or girl— guys can be on the receiving end of sexual harassment, too!) you dated starts ugly rumors about you, you can find yourself in a hostile environment, which falls under the heading of sexual harassment. If he writes something bad about you on the bathroom wall, you definitely have the right to report him to the principal—and to have the school do something about it. In fact, The Supreme Court of the United States has stated that a school can face a sex-discrimination suit for failing to intervene when a student complains of sexual harassment by another student.

You may find yourself the victim of sexual harassment in other ways too. For example, if you're walking down the hallway and someone tries to touch you inappropriately, or if someone constantly shouts obscenities at you—both these situations can

Dating with Confidence

be labeled harassment, and if you report them to your school principal, the kids doing it must be punished.

Some people still believe that behavior such as the type I've described is "to be expected" in school—that sometimes kids just act like idiots because they're kids, and there's nothing you can do about it. But if you feel uncomfortable or afraid when you're walking through the halls at school, then that's not just something to be expected or excused—it's something that must be dealt with.

If you are the victim of sexually harassing behavior, the best thing to do is tell your parents—let them know what's going on so they can help you take the next step. Second, report the incident to your school principal so it will be on the record, and so the school can have the opportunity to act. It might also be helpful to talk to your school counselor—he or she might have more information on the sexual harassment laws in your area.

Whatever you do, do not sit back and accept the behavior. And don't blame yourself, ever! Don't allow yourself to start thinking, "Well, maybe I did something to cause this" or "Maybe I did something on the date that gave him the wrong idea." The fact is, you did nothing to encourage this kind of behavior and you never deserve to be treated this way.

Remember that harassment can include:

- ✔ Unwanted touching
- ✔ Verbal comments and name-calling
- ✔ The spreading of sexual rumors
- ✔ Gestures, jokes, or cartoons
- ✔ Too-personal conversations or notes

Always remember that no one has to tolerate sexual harassment at school. Remember that there are adults you can trust who can help you.

THE FINAL WORD

It's not fun talking about serious issues like these, but it is necessary. Most of you will have perfectly wonderful dating experiences and won't ever need the information included in this chapter. But even if you never need it, it's good to have it stored in your memory, so you'll know what to do if something bad does happen when you're out on a date.

The most important thing to remember is this—prevention is always the best protection. If you take precautions and look out for yourself, you can avoid a bad situation, which is always easier than getting yourself out of one.

Some important tips to remember:

✔ Always let your parents or family members know exactly where you'll be. Leave a phone number if you can.

✔ Keep emergency money with you at all times so you can make phone calls or pay for a taxi when one is needed.

✔ Don't wander off alone with anyone you don't know well. If you're at a party or a social event with friends, let them know if you're going for a walk with your date. Also, let friends know when you're leaving the party. Don't ever just "disappear" on them.

✔ Talk to friends and adults you trust. If someone is treating you badly, let someone else know about it. You don't have to ever go through anything alone.

When It's All Over . . .

Your first date will be something you remember all your life. If you've followed the suggestions and tips I've given you in this book, you can be assured that you'll have an absolutely great time—or at least not the worst night of your life!

When your first date is over, and you've talked about it with your friends or your family, why not talk about it with yourself too? A nice way to remember your first date is to journal it. If you don't have a journal, this might be a good time to start one. Simply open the journal and start writing— you can write about how you felt, what happened, what went wrong, and what went right. You can make a note of things you want to remember for future dates. If it was bad, or boring, or silly, or just plain gross, you can write about that as well—how can you make it better the next time around? Did your date become a lot less "like-worthy"? Did he pick his teeth or hock up spit? Did she flirt with other guys at the party? Now you know better—this person was not the one for you.

Don't be discouraged if you have a bad date. Everyone has at least one, and believe me, it'll make for a great story one day. Journalizing, writing down what you liked and didn't like about your date, will give you a clearer idea of what exactly it is you're looking for in a person, and it'll give you a good picture of what you want future dates to be like.

And whatever you do, don't blame yourself if a date goes badly. Unless you acted like a real jerk (and you probably know if you did), it wasn't your fault—the two of you just weren't meant to be a couple. There are other people out there, people who share your interests and your values, who would love the chance to go out on a date with you, and don't you ever forget it!

Finally, remember that dating is supposed to be fun. It's a chance to get to know someone new, to make a new friend, and perhaps to experience a bit of romance. If your first date wasn't the greatest experience ever—if there were no bells and fireworks—just remember that your second, your third, or your twentieth could be the one that is.

CAN THIS BE LOVE?

So you had the time of your life on your first date. Your head is spinning and you're feeling like you're sitting on top of the world. Could this be love? Is it possible to fall head over feet on a first date?

Hey, stranger things have happened. But even though you might be thinking you've found the absolutely, positively best person ever, you should know that falling in love on a first date is a rare phenom.

Let's face it, many teens are totally into immediate gratification. They really want the world, and they really want it now. And lots of teenagers really want to fall in love.

There's also the whole "love at first sight" brigade who believe that you can fall for someone the second you meet them. It happens more than you might think—lots of happy couples will tell you they knew the second they met their partner that this was the person they were meant to be with. So it's definitely possible that this first date was enough to get your heart in love-gear.

But many times, teenagers think that because they had a great time on their date, and because they still think their like-object is pretty cool, it means they're in love. (This happens to people who are not teenagers as well—there are some things we don't grow out of and wanting to be in love is one of them!)

When it comes to love, remember to keep your wits about you. Don't start declaring your love and devotion the second your first date is over. You might be sure of what you're feeling, but your date may not be, and the best way to scare off an unsure like-object is to start shouting the "L" word at him or her.

Remember too that you're still young, and there are lots more people for you to meet and get to know. Even if you do have strong feelings for your date, there's still a possibility that there is another Mr. or Ms. Right waiting for you.

THE FIRST DATE–IT'S STILL ABOUT FUN

This book covered a lot of serious dating issues, but the bottom line is, when you're talking about a first date, you should be talking about something that's fun. It's fun to spend time with someone you like, and it's fun to do cool

TANYA'S STORY: TOO MUCH, TOO SOON

"I was fifteen when I went out on my first date with Brian. All my friends were already dating, and I was so excited that I had finally been asked out. He took me bowling, and then we went out to eat, and we had the best time ever. Everything was perfect, and we got along great together. I guess I must have gotten too excited, because when he brought me home and kissed me goodnight, I blurted out 'I love you!' He looked like I'd just punched him in the stomach! The next day, he barely spoke to me. When we finally sat down to talk about it, he told me that he'd had a great time too, but when I said 'I love you,' it freaked him out—and looking back, I can understand why. I mean, we were just starting to get to know one another. It was definitely a case of too much, too soon."

things together. If you had a good time on your first date, you've had a successful one. Once you get past the nerves and the anxiety, you have to admit that the reason people have been dating for decades is because dating is the best way to get to know someone special—and the best way to determine if that someone special is the right one for you. So enjoy your first date—and all your dates!

About the Author

Jackie Jarosz, editor of *SuperTeen* magazine is also a freelance writer who has written several books on teen celebrities, including Britney Spears and Christina Aguilera. She is also the author of the play *Last Call*, and is working on a movie screenplay. She lives in the New York City area with her husband, Arthur.

ALSO AVAILABLE FROM ADAMS MEDIA:

The Everything Dating Book
Leah and Elina Furman

Trade paperback, $12.95
ISBN: 1-58062-185-6

Looking for romance? *The Everything Dating Book* will help you find it. Quirky and unpredictable, exciting and surprising, dating can be the best part of your "singles" life. Experts Leah and Elina Furman provide everything you need to know—how to look your best and feel great, meet people who are just right for you, plan unforgettable dates, and more! Loaded with essential information, *The Everything Dating Book* features dozens of clever tips, helpful quizzes, handy checklists, and illuminating anecdotes about real dating situations. Filled with savvy, funny straight talk featuring valuable lessons from planning the first date to celebrating Valentine's Day, *The Everything Dating Book* puts you on the road to romance!

See the entire Everything series at www.adamsmedia.com/everything

Available wherever books are sold.

**For more information, or to order, call 800-872-5627
or visit www.adamsmedia.com**

Adams Media Corporation, 260 Center Street, Holbrook, MA 02343

ALSO AVAILABLE FROM ADAMS MEDIA:

Dating:
A Survival Guide from the Front Lines
Josey Vogels

Trade paperback, $9.95
ISBN: 1-58062-176-7

Punchy and provocative, forthright and funny as hell, sex and relationships diva Josey Vogels tells it like it is in this hard-hitting, entertaining and enlightening look at dating in the "age of the jaded." From first impressions to first-date foibles, one-liners to one-night stands, Dating delivers savvy tips, lively insight and downright good advice on the often frustrating, but always fascinating, art of coupling.

Available wherever books are sold.
**For more information, or to order, call 800-872-5627
or visit www.adamsmedia.com**
Adams Media Corporation, 260 Center Street, Holbrook, MA 02343